MY
WISHES

MY WISHES

Your Plan
for Communicating and Organizing
the Essential Information
Your Family Needs

Benjamin Berkley

Attorney at Law

SPHINX® PUBLISHING
AN IMPRINT OF SOURCEBOOKS, INC.®
NAPERVILLE, ILLINOIS
www.SphinxLegal.com

First Edition: 2006

Published by: **Sphinx® Publishing, An Imprint of Sourcebooks, Inc.®**
Naperville Office
P.O. Box 4410
Naperville, Illinois 60567-4410
630-961-3900
Fax: 630-961-2168
www.sourcebooks.com
www.SphinxLegal.com

This publication is designed to provide accurate and authoritative information in regard to the subject matter covered. It is sold with the understanding that the publisher is not engaged in rendering legal, accounting, or other professional service. If legal advice or other expert assistance is required, the services of a competent professional person should be sought.

From a Declaration of Principles Jointly Adopted by a Committee of the American Bar Association and a Committee of Publishers and Associations

This product is not a substitute for legal advice.

Disclaimer required by Texas statutes.

Library of Congress Cataloging-in-Publication Data
Berkley, Benjamin.
    My wishes : your plan for communicating and organizing the essential information your family needs / by Benjamin Berkley.
        p. cm.
    ISBN-13: 978-1-57248-519-8 (pbk. : alk. paper)
    ISBN-10: 1-57248-519-1 (pbk. : alk. paper)
    1. Estate planning--United States--Popular works. I. Title.

KF750.Z9B472 2006
332.024'016--dc22

2006007035

Printed and bound in the United States of America.
SB — 10 9 8 7 6 5 4 3 2 1

To my beautiful family—my wife, Phyllis, and my children, Cliff and Allison. Thanks for all your love and support, and for always making me smile.

To the memory of my father, with all my love and respect.

To my high school teacher and mentor, Thomas Lovely. You gave me the wisdom to find the words.

And to my Uncle Milton. The case is closed!

CONTENTS

Chapter 3: Advance Health Care Planning and Organ Donation 15

Chapter 4: The Role of Hospice 25

Chapter 5: The Funeral Service 29

Chapter 6: Preplanning Arrangements 41

PREFACE

When I announced to my wife that I was writing this book, she replied, "Why not a love story, or a book on travel? This is gruesome." She went on to say that she would never buy such a book. Her response is typical of how most people first react to the thought of someday not being here. We live in a society where dying is not freely discussed. No one wants to think about it—let alone plan for it—but dying is inevitable. It is something we all must face. The goal, of course, is to put off the event as long as possible. However, planning for the inevitable needs to be a part of your life.

As background, I have practiced law for over twenty-eight years with an emphasis on probate and estate planning. When I consult with a client for estate planning, I discuss the benefits of a Will and other legal documents. I also inquire whether any arrangements have been made with regards to funeral and final interment, as well as disposition of personal property. I further question if any family members are aware of the location of important papers. Often, the client jokingly replies, "It doesn't matter. When I am no longer here, then it's their problem." The "their" usually refers to surviving children. However, after I describe the importance of this type of planning and explain the options available, the client decides to start putting things in order.

Unfortunately, too often I receive calls from family members whose parents did not put something in order. Many people prepare estate planning documents, but neglect to tell their children how to locate all of the bank accounts, deeds, insurance policies, and other important papers. A mourning spouse or child is now faced with mounting bills and expenses related to the decedent's last illness and no idea how to pay them.

Accepting that someone is no longer here is devastating. To then confront the decisions and arrangements that must be addressed can be emotionally exhausting. Though we protect our home from an approaching storm, or make arrangements to have the mail taken in when we are away, planning for our passing is something we continually put off. As a result, an unprepared family may face serious financial and psychological consequences.

In my many years of practice, I have repeatedly seen how the loss of a loved one has wreaked havoc on a family. Sudden death is most devastating, as there is often no planning in place. However, even when a patient is terminally ill, the family often avoids any conversation of making final plans. In preparing this book, I questioned many clients who suffered the loss of a loved one as to why the subject was avoided. Though a small percentage responded that they always held out hope that there would be a cure, the majority answered that they could not bear to think of the inevitable.

Death and dying are becoming increasingly relevant for baby boomers. With approximately 2.4 million Americans dying each year—and the number growing—it is only logical that thoughtful, serious, and personal conversations take place with friends and loved ones so that you are well prepared for the end of life. The time to take charge is before you encounter a life-threatening illness or crisis. This will greatly reduce the stress endured by your survivors. By preparing in advance, you can alleviate some of the uncertainty and anxiety survivors experience when they do not know what you would have wanted.

Dying is no laughing matter. However, in discussing the subject matter, it does not have to be presented in a depressing form. Accordingly, by blending experience learned from my clients, anecdotes where appropriate, and a sprinkling of humor, *My Wishes* explores all the issues facing one's passing. Most important, the reader who follows this handbook will gain a sense of security knowing that his or her affairs will be in order.

Finally, *My Wishes* is a planning guide, offering practical information for you and your loved ones. It is not meant to depress, but instead, to inspire. It provides for an orderly transition for the survivors, and helps avoid both the financial and psychological burdens that often become the responsibilities of the survivors. Equally as important, it provides peace of mind for you and your loved ones. You owe it to yourself and those you care for to be prepared.

Many of us have, unfortunately, experienced the loss of a loved one. Sometimes we learn after the passing of a loved one what his or her last wishes were. If you have a story or an experience that you would like to share for a future edition of this book, please go to **www.mywishesthebook.com** and click the link "my stories." All stories and experiences will be considered for future publication.

—*Ben Berkley*

INTRODUCTION

My Wishes is a planning guide. The purpose of the book is to provide practical information for you and your loved ones. A person does not have to be facing imminent death for the book to be relevant. Instead, this material should be viewed as a resource guide to put an orderly plan in place. Further, the book is intended as a reference. As a reference guide, it does not have to be read cover to cover.

The book discusses end of life issues, including:

➤ preparing for sudden death;

➤ advance health care planning and powers of attorney;

➤ how to behave towards others when you are ill;

➤ preparing a message to your children on how to behave with each other after you are no longer here;

➤ hospice care;

➤ Wills, Trusts, estate planning, and asset protection;

➤ financial planning;

➤ arranging for your pets after you are gone;

➤ pre-need arrangements and funeral planning;

➤ writing your own eulogy and Legacy Will;

➤ disposing of personal property;

➤ embracing your spirituality;

➤ managing debt;

➤ Social Security disability and other federal insurance programs;
➤ unfinished business, including future purchases and claims you may have against others; and,
➤ issues faced by partners of a same-sex relationship.

The book is divided into two parts.

PART 1—PERSONAL ISSUES

Chapter 1 discusses what happens when one passes suddenly without any planning. It illustrates how the survivors are often unprepared for the inevitable and why it is prudent to have a plan in place. It includes a financial planning checklist if you become terminally ill. It also discusses enjoying life to the fullest. Chapter 2 discusses what steps you need to take to continue living while you plan for the inevitable.

In Chapter 3, you will learn about the importance of making decisions about advance health care planning, end of life treatment options, and organ donation. Chapter 4 discusses hospice care and the requirements needed to qualify for benefits.

Chapter 5 provides a guide to planning your funeral service. It is becoming more common for people to make pre-need arrangements for their funeral and final interment, and Chapter 6 discusses these arrangements. It also discusses final interment options. You may want to write your own eulogy and tape a video message for your loved ones. Options for doing so appear in Chapter 7.

Chapter 8 discusses the issues that must be addressed if you have to relocate from your home due to illness or other reasons. It provides information on senior living housing options that are available. Chapter 9 discusses issues faced by people who live alone.

Chapter 10 is a discussion about your behavior towards others and a parent's message to children on how to behave with each other after a parent passes away. A traditional Will disposes of property, but the Legacy Will discussed in Chapter 11 is your written expression to your family and friends of who you are, how you wish to be remembered, and what lessons you want to leave.

PART 2—MANAGING YOUR AFFAIRS

A discussion of distributing and disposing of your personal property and what a Will does not cover is provided in Chapter 12. This chapter also discusses how to arrange care for your pets after your passing.

Chapter 13 discusses the differences between Wills and Trusts and whether you need one. Chapter 14 addresses the importance of Living Wills. Chapter 15 describes Health Care and Financial Powers of Attorney, as well as special situations like appointing guardians of your children and protecting your same-sex relationship.

Chapter 16 discusses canceling credit card accounts, paying bills, and providing computer access to your passwords so that your survivors can obtain your information. Often, a medical crisis makes it very difficult to manage your everyday bills when you have medical bills to pay, and Chapter 17 provides advice on how to manage such a situation.

Chapter 18 includes a discussion of private insurance options, including disability, long-term care, and funeral insurance. It also discusses reverse mortgages. Information about federal insurance benefit programs, including Social Security disability and veteran's benefits, can be found in Chapter 19.

Chapter 20 discusses the role of an attorney in drafting estate planning documents and providing consultation on end-of-life issues.

You can learn how to avoid scam artists who prey on people's vulnerabilities during periods of stress in Chapter 21.

Chapter 22 discusses notification and instructions to others upon your passing. Chapter 23 discusses unfinished business, such as purchases and other contracts that you may have entered into that may not be completed before your passing, as well as claims you may have against others and how the claims may be continued on behalf of your estate.

Following the Conclusion is a glossary of the most commonly used terms. Finally, the appendix contains useful forms for planning for the inevitable.

Please note that laws vary from state to state. As such, it is advisable to consult with an attorney or visit a law library to be sure that the form is correct for your needs. If you would like to read the laws themselves, you may want to check out Gavel2Gavel, an Internet resource providing every state's codes and statutes. The direct link is **www.request.net/ g2g/codes/state/index.htm**. Simply click on your state's name, and you will be directed to the codes and statutes for your state.

Blank forms are provided throughout the book. Jot down notes to yourself on these pages as you read the book. The forms also appear in the appendix. Use your notes from earlier to fill out and keep these forms from the appendix.

PART 1
PERSONAL ISSUES

CHAPTER 1:
PREPARING FOR THE INEVITABLE

As children, we believe we are invincible. We can ski the steepest mountain and challenge the highest wave. When we are young, sleep, diet, and exercise often take a back seat to having fun. However, upon the passing of a loved one, we are forced to face our own mortality. There is never a right age for being able to accept that someone has passed away or that we, too, will be gone someday. However, it is important to face these facts and plan for that unfortunate and often sudden event, so that when tragedy strikes, your survivors do not find themselves scrambling to find the pieces of the puzzle that were held by you.

Ben's Story

My father died suddenly at age 59. We had spoken by phone the day before. The conversation was typical—we chatted about our New York Yankees, the weather, and the stock market. He was feeling fine and there was no reason to believe that twenty-four hours later, he would be gone. Like many families of my parents' generation, the husband wrote the checks and paid the bills. My mom was overwhelmed with emotion and terribly unprepared for life after my dad's passing.

The events of September 11, 2001 are a sobering reminder that we never know when the end will come. Of the more than 2,000 people who perished that day, the great majority had no arrangements in place for the unthinkable. They kissed their wives, husbands, and children good-bye that morning, never thinking that day was their last day on Earth. For weeks, the news was filled with stories of surviving families facing financial disaster as a result of the terrible disruption. Insurance companies could not issue death benefits because insurance policies could not be located. Families who needed to sell their homes often had to seek court permission, because people whose names were on the titles were no longer here to sign deeds to transfer titles.

Jane's Story

Several years ago, a frantic woman called my office. Jane's husband had died. She knew he had insurance, but she could not locate the insurance policy, even though she had turned the house upside down. At the time of his passing, the couple was overextended in debt. Creditors were calling and their bank was threatening to foreclose on their home, since they were three months behind in payments. With my assistance, the insurance company finally issued a check for the insurance benefits after Jane signed a declaration that the insurance policy was lost or destroyed. Unfortunately, by the time the company performed payment, Jane's home was scheduled to be sold at a foreclosure sale.

By planning for the inevitable, you are taking the first steps in protecting the future lives of your loved ones when you are no longer here. It is prudent to be prepared in order to avoid the disruption that is often faced by your survivors upon your passing.

Planning for the Inevitable—Presidential Style

Days after President Reagan had passed away, a *Los Angeles Times* article provided information about the advanced planning for his passing. In fact, within days after he was sworn in as the nation's fortieth president in 1981, Reagan and his wife Nancy began discussing funeral arrangements for if he were to die in office.

According to the article, Mr. Reagan chose the music that he wanted to be played at his funeral service. He and Nancy also selected the verses and psalms to be recited. The details even included the names of the pall-bearers he wished to have the honor of carrying his casket and the number of times "Hail to the Chief" would be performed.

Every year thereafter, the plans were reviewed and revised. After he left office in 1988, Reagan appointed a committee that was part of his presidential library to oversee the funeral arrangements, though he continued to be consulted regarding all details. In the mid-1990s, after his medical condition prevented him from partaking in any discussions, his family continued to provide input.

When Reagan died in June of 2004, his family was well prepared for the inevitable. Of course, only presidents and other dignitaries are afforded funerals where their bodies lie in state in the Capitol Rotunda and require such precise planning. However, it should not be minimized that proper planning reduces the emotional strain on your loved ones when you are no longer here, no matter who you are.

Sudden Adult Death

Some of the most difficult calls I have taken over the years have been from grieving family members who found my business card in the personal phone book of their recently deceased loved one with the words "call in the event of my death" written on it.

One of the most common, and emotionally difficult, forms of passing is sudden adult death. When a loved one dies suddenly and for no apparent reason, it is often more devastating than if the loved one had been ill, because the survivors have had no time to emotionally prepare. Survivors are sometimes wracked with guilt, especially if their last conversation with their loved one was not pleasant. Still, after the grieving and the soul-searching, the survivors must begin the task of learning how to survive without their loved one. This includes funeral and financial arrangements, which will be much easier to complete if you have done some planning for the inevitable.

The recent South Asian tsunami disaster is an unfortunate illustration of sudden death, and of how tragedy can strike at any time without warning. The monster waves destroyed everything in their path. When I watched in horror the home videos taken by tourists, I vividly remembered walking with my family on the beautiful beaches of Phuket, Thailand. My thoughts immediately went to the families of those who had died. They are the survivors who had no warning or time to prepare for the loss of a loved one. They must now address both the emotional and legal issues associated with their loss. This task becomes even more difficult if no plan was in place for the inevitable.

Terminal Illness

The five most dreaded words a doctor can say to a patient are "I have some bad news." Any conversation that follows is usually a blur ending with the suggestion to get affairs in order.

Receiving such devastating news is impossible to comprehend. However, it is information that is meant to stimulate action and not inaction. The message is not to wait too long to organize your affairs—do this before you reach a point where you can no longer do things for yourself.

Many people, after receiving such news, are anxious to complete their estate planning needs. They understand that their time remaining is precious and that there is an urgency to attend to these affairs. Clients often tell me that until their estate planning needs are complete, they cannot plan for the time remaining.

Unfortunately, some people wait too long and are no longer competent to make decisions by the time they decide to sign the important papers. As a result, a lawyer cannot prepare documents, because the lawyer must know that the client understands the document. Also, most documents must be witnessed by at least two impartial individuals who attest or sign in writing that the person was of sound mind, and was not acting under duress or undue influence. If the maker of a Will, for example, is not competent due to being under the influence of medication, the Will can later be challenged.

Jill's Story

I received a call from Jill, who asked if I would visit her ill father. She said Bob was having difficulty speaking but could communicate in an audible whisper. Upon my arrival, I observed that Bob was on an intravenous line for pain and was almost comatose. Needless to say, I could not consult with him. Unfortunately, Bob passed away without a Will. His estate, which included a four-plex residential property and other savings, had to be probated. The estate paid over $20,000 in probate and attorney's fees. Bob could have prevented his estate's eventual legal consequences and fees had he consulted with an attorney for proper estate planning when he was diagnosed with lung cancer a year earlier.

Live Life Today

Finally, planning for the inevitable includes living for today. You need to put your financial and end-of-life affairs in order, but it is important that you also consider how you want to spend your time and money on this Earth. Consider taking that dream vacation or that exciting new job. It is said that the only two guarantees in life are death and taxes, so you might as well live life for today. Time passes us by very quickly, and living in a world where time is so compressed and schedules are constantly being juggled to fit in as much as possible sometimes causes us to lose sight of why we are here.

I am often asked by clients to give what I would consider nonlegal advice. The tough questions are from those who are facing a terminal illness. There is still that part of them that wants to explore the Amazon or challenge the highest mountain. Should he and his wife go on the Mediterranean cruise that was to be their 50th wedding anniversary present to each other? Should she take all the grandchildren to Disney World now instead of waiting until school is out? I wish that someone had told my father not to put off visiting Israel until his retirement. When he died suddenly at age 59, he had never fulfilled his dream.

There are no answers to these questions, and I can only offer support and hope. But from client experiences, I can attest that every client who said "I am going to live life today" never regretted that he or she did!

Ralph's Story

Recently, Ralph and his girlfriend Alice retained my services. During the consultation, Ralph informed me that he had inoperable stomach cancer. His doctor told him that the tumors had spread and that he had a few weeks to live. He was only 35 years old. Neither Ralph nor Alice had been married before, but they were madly in love and wanted to know if I thought they should marry. They wanted to share whatever time Ralph had left together as husband and wife. After counseling them on the legal ramifications of marriage, I told them if they invited me to their wedding, I would come. It was a great party and we danced our feet off.

Living life today is not limited to doing and going. As my clients have shown me, living life today includes giving today. Whether it is writing a check to a charity, dropping a few coins in the Salvation Army kettle, or making an offering in church on Sunday, you may realize joy by giving during your lifetime from the estate that you have worked so hard to amass.

Federal tax law generally allows an individual to give up to $12,000 per year to anyone without paying gift taxes. That means you can transfer some of your wealth to your children or others during your lifetime to reduce your taxable estate. For example, you could give $12,000 a year to each of your children and grandchildren, and your spouse could do likewise (for a total of $24,000 per year to each child). As a result, by reducing the overall value of your estate, your estate will owe less to the IRS for estate taxes upon your passing. In deciding whether to make a monetary gift to a relative, you should first consult with your tax consultant.

Mary's Story

Mary asked me to review her Will. She did not have a large estate from a dollar value, but she had a vast collection of porcelain dolls. Her granddaughters always played with them when they visited. Her Will listed each grandchild and the figurine dolls they were to receive. Mary wanted to delete the mention of the dolls. Instead, she wanted to give the dolls to her grandchildren now, during her lifetime. She said she wanted to experience the joy of seeing her grandchildren enjoy the gifts.

A Financial Planning Checklist for Terminal Illness

The emotional issues involved with the news that you or a loved one is terminally ill are devastating, but it is critical to address the financial issues as well. The following is a checklist of some of the financial issues that need to be addressed by you and your family if you have been diagnosed with a terminal illness. These topics are more fully discussed in Part 2 of this book.

- ○ **Start planning immediately.** Though you may be in denial, time is of the essence. Also, proper planning may relieve apprehension.
- ○ **Determine what costs should be expected with the illness.** Talk to your doctors, and get information about medical expenses and other costs associated with assisted living.
- ○ **Prepare a budget.** Include in your budget additional medical costs and any special wishes that you may have, such as a dream vacation.

○ **Decide whether to keep working.** Work may provide critical financial, medical, and psychological benefits. However, consider changing to a less demanding job.

○ **Review health insurance.** Is your illness a preexisting condition that is not covered under your present policy? What are the lifetime maximum benefits? How much must you pay out of pocket? Will it cover experimental treatments? Will your coverage expire? You must review your health insurance policy so you can answer these questions, and adjust your plan based on those answers.

○ **Review disability insurance.** Is there disability insurance through work or is a personal policy available? What percentage of your income will it replace? What is the waiting period before benefits begin? Are the benefits taxable? Are there are any state sources available? Knowing these answers will help you complete your planning.

○ **Establish care.** Where are you likely to go for care? Your home? A nursing home? The hospital? A hospice care facility? Can family members help at home? Each option has associated costs to consider.

○ **Review life insurance.** You may be able to borrow against the cash value of whole life insurance. This is not applicable for term life insurance. The policy may also pay what is called *accelerated benefits*, or the policy may be sold to a third party in what is called a *viatical settlement*. These living benefits pay in cash a percentage (usually 30% to 90%) of the death benefits.

○ **Review your investments.** It may be in your and your family's best interest to move assets like stocks and bonds into more liquid investments, such as money market accounts, as there is a lesser degree of risk involved.

○ **Assess other assets.** Is money available from 401(k)s, IRAs, or equity in property? Consider reverse mortgages.

○ **Review government sources.** People with few assets and little income usually qualify for Medicare to pay nursing home care. Medicare can also pay for hospice care. Social Security disability income may be available if you have worked five of the last ten years prior to your illness and had Social Security withholdings taken from your paycheck.

○ **Consider tax issues.** Many of these checklist items, such as withdrawals from IRAs or sales of investment items, may pose tax-planning issues that need to be discussed with your tax consultant.

○ **Draft or update estate planning documents.** Every adult should have a Will. Consider drafting other documents, such as powers of attorney and a Living Will, as well. A Durable Power of Attorney lets you appoint someone to make financial decisions for you. A Living Will describes what life-saving medical treatment you may or may not want. A Health Care Power of Attorney appoints someone you trust to make medical decisions if you are unable to do so yourself.

○ **Review beneficiaries.** Be sure the names of beneficiaries are up to date in your Will, insurance policies, and retirement plans.

○ **Hire professional help.** An estate-planning attorney and other financial professionals can be of immense help in making sure that the best plan is created and carried out.

CHAPTER 2:
LIVING WITH DYING

Part of planning for the inevitable includes learning how to live the remainder of your life knowing that you are dying. If you are diagnosed with a terminal illness, there are some special planning needs you should follow.

Your acknowledgment that you are dying is the first step to living with dying. This becomes even more of a challenge when your diagnosis comes without warning and is completely unexpected. If you are feeling great with no physical symptoms, the news is psychologically devastating.

Mike's Story

Mike had a routine physical for a new job. A chest x-ray revealed a suspicious nodule, and a follow-up CT scan found a tumor that was later determined to be of a very aggressive type of cancer. A month earlier he had competed in his fifth marathon run and was the picture of perfect health. He thought he had plenty of time to get things in order despite his doctor's advice, so he did not immediately draft any estate planning documents. He died a month later without making any last wishes arrangements.

Accepting Fate—Not Death

By accepting your fate, you are not letting go of hope. Acknowledging the reality of your fate, instead of denying it, makes the planning process easier. Planning for the inevitable is intended to make life easier and less stressful for your survivors after you have passed.

No two people process the news of a terminal illness the same way. Your initial reaction may be that of anger, denial, or hope. Your emotions must be addressed accordingly. However, when you are facing the most difficult challenge of your life, you must separate emotions from logic. This book's intent is to be a resource guide for logic so that you can put the necessary groundwork for your loved ones to follow into place.

Getting in tune with your emotional state of mind will help you live with your illness. You must be in control and never let others tell you how you feel. Remember that there is no right or wrong way for you to think or feel. What is important for you to remember is to stay focused on your agenda—putting your life in order so that your survivors may avoid suffering stress and financial harm.

Finding the Support You Need

It is during this most difficult time in your life that your family and friends must respect your needs and wishes. There will be times when you do not want to talk about your illness. There will also be periods when you may want to talk only to some people and exclude others. Regardless, if you make your thoughts and feelings known, you are more likely to receive the kind of care and companionship that will be most helpful to you. Remember, if you do not want to talk about your illness, do not feel that you have to. You must be in control.

Part of planning for the inevitable includes informing your family and friends of your terminal illness. How your survivors process the news differs with each individual and the relationship that you have with that person. Many will be shocked. Many will cry. Some will refuse to believe it while others will spring into action—offering to run errands, organize your home, cook meals, and do just about anything. There are also those who will not know how to respond or express themselves to you. They may fear for their own mortality and will avoid you altogether. Keep in mind that their apparent abandonment does not mean they do not care.

It is important that you listen to your body. As your illness progresses, you may become fatigued. Likewise, your strength and ability to make decisions and think clearly may become impaired. Respect what your mind and body are telling you, but do not put off organizing your affairs.

Planning for the inevitable also includes saying good-bye to those you care about. There is no time during your illness that is the right time to say good-bye, but you will know when it is right. Depending upon your abilities, you might want to set aside time to talk one-on-one or have a gathering for friends and family. Other ways of communicating include writing letters and creating videotapes. (see Chapter 7.)

Mark's Story

Several years ago, I received a call from an old high school friend. Though we had seen each other at the school reunions, we never stayed in touch. I was happy to hear from Mark and assumed he looked me up because he was planning a trip to California. Unfortunately, the reason for his call was not so pleasant. Mark had been diagnosed with leukemia. He took an early retirement from his job and wanted to contact his old high school buddies to say good-bye. Upon hearing the news, I immediately responded with all the trite remarks like "I am so sorry" and "How can this be?" However, Mark did not want to dwell on the prognosis. He wanted to reminisce about the old days. As his friend, I respected his wishes.

Part of the planning process includes reaching out for support. This is not the time to cling foolishly to an independence that is no longer possible. Even if you have always lived your life doing everything on your own, your illness may progress to a point where you will need help. As difficult as it may be for you, you must reach out. Of course, family and friends will be there for you, but you may want to consider hospice care. (see Chapter 4.) Hospice workers are trained to help both you and your survivors. For more information on hospice care, go to the Hospice Foundation of America website at **www.hospicefoundation.org**, and the website for the National Hospice and Palliative Care Organization at **www.nhpco.org**.

In the song "That's What Friends Are For," the lyrics suggest that a friend will always be there for you. However, there may be times when you do not want to be visited by your friends. If you are ill, it is important for those around you to respect your wishes. It is perfectly permissible to let your family or whomever you appoint to know the names of those you wish to see and those you do not. Remember, a really true friend will not have his or her feelings ruffled.

Embracing Your Spirituality

If faith has been a part of your life, the strength you have received from your beliefs should provide comfort now. Reading spiritual books, attending religious services, and surrounding yourself with people who share your beliefs will provide support.

If you want to seek spiritual guidance, find someone who will not be critical and will allow you to explore your feelings. Talk to your spiritual leader. If you are not affiliated with any particular church or synagogue, hospice care organizations can make referrals to you. You can also search your local Yellow Pages under the category "Grief Counselors."

Joe's Story

I once consulted with a gentleman who was dying of AIDS and wanted to make a Will. When Joe revealed to his family that he was gay, his wife divorced him and would not allow him to have a relationship with his kids. He desperately needed to talk to someone, as he felt so alone in this world. A friend of mine who does grief counseling befriended Joe and provided the professional support that he so needed.

CHAPTER 3:
ADVANCE HEALTH CARE PLANNING AND ORGAN DONATION

We make plans for special events like milestone birthdays, weddings, and summer vacations. It is equally important to plan for the health care you may want if you were to become terminally ill. Advance care planning includes talking with your loved ones and putting your wishes in writing. By having a plan in place for your advance care wishes, your can live well, knowing you are prepared. Decisions for advance care are best made before you are ill, but you may make changes as the years go by.

PRACTICAL POINT
All of us make health care choices during our lives. Regardless of the state of your present health, an accident or serious illness can occur. Preparing for such a change is important for everyone, no matter how old or young. Talking about your choices is a part of advance care planning. Your family's assumption of what you want may be wrong.

The following scenarios help illustrate the value of advance health care planning.

➤ Yesterday, you played two hard sets of tennis. Today, you are suddenly critically ill. Treatment decisions need to be made, but you are too sick to make them alone.

➤ You were involved in a terrible car accident resulting in brain injury and have been on life support for ten days. The doctor has told your family that there is no chance of recovery. Your family cannot agree on whether to turn off the machines.

➤ You have cancer of the esophagus, and are having trouble speaking and swallowing. You must weigh the risks and benefits of a feeding tube, but have never expressed to your family whether you would want one inserted.

Bill's Story

There is good reason for the saying "never put off for tomorrow what you can do today." A prospective client had called me to set up an appointment for a Trust. Bill was separated from his wife and had two small children. He was always traveling, and scheduling time was difficult. Due to other commitments, Bill rescheduled his appointment four times. Prior to his last scheduled appointment, he was seriously injured in a head-on car collision. For weeks, his estranged wife and her in-laws fought over the decisions for his health care while he lay in a coma.

Develop a Plan

Once you have determined your health care choices, it is important that you develop a plan for choosing the setting for your care. In other words, where do you wish to live as you approach the end of life? You may choose to receive end-of-life care at:

➤ home;

➤ a nursing home;

➤ an assisted living facility;

➤ home or a nursing home, with hospice care;

➤ a hospice residence; or,

➤ a hospital.

Share Your Plan

Part of advance health care planning includes talking about your decisions with loved ones and your doctors. Your decisions need not be made alone. Talking about these subjects with loved ones can create stronger bonds with them. Still, it is not always easy to start the conversation. One way to start is by sharing the reason for making advance health care decisions. You can say something like the following.

> *We never know when our time to die will come, but we all know it is coming. I want to share my thoughts with you so that you don't have to make decisions without knowing what I want. Please ask me what I want as long as I am able to think and express myself. I just want you to be prepared to speak for me if I can't speak for myself.*

The following are some other suggestions for starting this conversation.

➤ *Refer to a book or movie that you found thought-provoking.* "I watched *On Golden Pond* the other night and it made me think about my own death. I have some ideas about how I want it to be, so I have started to prepare for that time, whenever it comes. I want to share these thoughts with you and hear what you have to say about it."

➤ *Refer to a situation that your family will know.* "I have been thinking about what Joan has been going through in the hospital. Her family is under so much stress because they don't know what to do. Would she continue the ventilator if it were up to her? I don't want you to have to make a treatment decision for me without knowing what I want."

➤ *Have a matter-of-fact conversation within the context of legal or business preparation.* "I am taking care of some matters that have to do with my will, my belongings, and my health care. I would like to talk with you about my wishes for how medical decisions will be made if needed. If I were unable to make decisions for myself, I need to know if you would be able and willing to speak for me."

When having such conversations, your children will typically interrupt you by saying, "I don't want to hear about it. This is morbid. You're going to be here forever. Can we please talk about something else?" Do not be concerned, because they did hear what you said and will remember your wishes.

If you have a life-threatening illness, it is also important that you talk to your doctor about the kind of care you want at the end of your life. This is best done when you are able to think clearly, and make and communicate your plan. Talk with your doctor about your current health, as well as the possible health situations and choices you may face in the future, given the nature of your illness. Your doctor should be pleased that you are bringing up this topic. Ask if he or she will advise you on your advance care plan and honor your plan. The following are some questions that are useful to discuss with your doctor if your health worsens or if you have a serious illness.

> ➤ What is my diagnosis, and how serious is it?
> ➤ What usually happens with an illness like mine?
> ➤ How long might I have to live?
> ➤ What are my options for treatment?
> ➤ What are the benefits and risks of each option?

Treatment Issues

When death is approaching, there are treatments that can alter the dying process. Ask your doctor about the goal of any treatment and consider which treatments you might want.

You may choose to try a treatment for a limited period of time, until your condition improves or doctors decide that the treatment does not work. Alternately, you may want to try to live as long as possible, with medical technology prolonging your life. If you prefer that treatment not be used to prolong your life, you should be clear about this wish and ask that treatment only be used to ensure your comfort.

David Chapman, MD, is an internist and gastroenterologist. Many of his patients are elderly, and he has been asked on numerous occasions to help develop end-of-life treatment options. Dr. Chapman suggests you discuss the following options with your doctor.

> ➤ *Antibiotics* are medications given to fight infections. They will not reverse the primary condition of a terminally ill patient. Antibiotics may help reduce discomfort caused by an infection, although comfort measure may also provide relief. Earlier in the course of a terminal illness, antibiotics can cure an infection and give you more time to enjoy life.

> *Artificial hydration and nutrition* can be given when you can no longer eat or drink enough to stay alive. Intravenous (IV) fluids are given into a vein. Liquid feeding is administered through a feeding tube in your nose or stomach. As the body gradually shuts down, however, nutrition is no longer necessary to maintain comfort. The body no longer suffers hunger pains. It desires only moisture for the mouth to be comfortable.

> *Blood transfusions* may be helpful in boosting your energy while you still have quality of life despite a terminal illness. Later in a terminal illness, blood transfusions will not result in relief of symptoms.

> *Cardiopulmonary resuscitation* (CPR) can be attempted if your heart or breathing should stop. CPR is a group of procedures performed on a person whose heart stops beating or who stops breathing. If you were outside a hospital, it is likely you would be taken to a hospital, and if necessary, attached to a ventilator or breathing machine. CPR is usually successful in reviving someone who is elderly, terminally ill, or critically ill.

> *Do not hospitalize orders* can be written for nursing home residents who may experience a more comfortable death in a familiar environment. If you have not specified your wishes while you are still competent, it becomes the responsibility of the family member to initiate such a request. Failure to consider the likely eventuality that the patient will develop another acute illness is the most common reason for repeated, unpleasant, and ultimately futile re-hospitalizations.

> *Do not resuscitate orders* (DNRs) can prevent medical workers from applying CPR or electrical shocks when death occurs inside a medical facility. A DNR is a doctor's order in your medical records that says you do not want to be revived if your heart or breathing stops.

> *Do not intubate orders* (DNIs) are similar to DNRs, and mean that you will not have a tube inserted into your throat and lungs, and will not be put on a ventilator.

> *Pain management* with excellent pain medications is available to control most pain. Some of these may cause sleepiness, though the side effect may go away after you become used to the medication. You may want to remain as alert as possible, or you may want maximum pain control. Talk to your doctor, as either may be possible.

> *Surgery* or other procedures at the end of life are often not appropriate unless they are specifically for comfort and other treatments have not been effective in relieving symptoms.

> *Symptom control* may be necessary when dealing with end-of-life illnesses. Symptoms such as pain, shortness of breath, nausea, or anxiety are sometimes part of the dying process. You may request a doctor or nurse who is skilled in palliative care.

PRACTICAL POINT

If you are not able to make decisions and have not named someone to make medical decisions for you, state laws vary as to who can make decisions for you. In most states, your spouse has the authority to make decisions for you if you cannot. If you are in a committed same-sex relationship, appointing your partner with the authority to make both financial and health care decisions for you avoids a challenge from a family member seeking to make those decisions. (see Chapter 15.)

Chapters 14 and 15 provides information about drafting a Living Will and an Advance Health Care Power of Attorney, with samples of each. An Advance Health Care Planning Worksheet can be found in that chapter on page 23.

Organ Donation

Donating your organs upon your passing requires advanced planning. Unfortunately, many people want to donate but do not take the necessary steps in advance of their passing. As a result, many organs that could be transplanted to save lives are never used.

Since the demand for organs far exceeds supply, federal and state governments have imposed very strict laws aimed at increasing donations. In fact, many states have passed legislation that requires hospitals to ask patients if they would like to complete an organ donation card.

Organ donations are legally referred to as *anatomical gifts*. All fifty states have laws regarding organ donation. The federal government has passed the *Uniform Anatomical Gift Act*, which allows a person to donate organs and tissues to be used for transplantation, therapy, research, and medical education.

NOTE: Organs and tissues may not always be suitable for donation. For example, if someone died of a highly infectious disease, his or her organs may not be acceptable for donation.

If it is your wish to be an organ donor, you have several options. You may carry a donor card with you. Donor cards are available from national organizations such as the National Kidney Foundation. Some states provide check boxes to elect organ donation on your driver's license renewal or application. If you elect to be a donor, that information is printed on your driver's license. By contacting your local hospital, your health care provider, or your state's organ procurement organization, you can learn of methods available in your state for organ donation.

You may also contact the national Coalition on Donation at 804-782-4920 or visit **www.shareyourlife.org** to request a donor card. The Coalition on Donation can also provide the phone number and contact information for the local organ and tissue recovery organization that serves your area. To find an eye bank near you and to request an eye donor card, you can call the Eye Bank Association of America at 202-775-4999 or visit **www.restoresight.org**.

PRACTICAL POINT

Organ donations can also be indicated in a document known as an *Advance Health Care Directive.* (see Chapter 15.) Because such instructions might not be read in time to allow organs or tissues to be donated, it is important that your family and loved ones know of your desire to donate. Planning for such a possibility and making your decisions known in advance increases the likelihood that your wishes will be followed upon your death.

Revoking Organ Donations

If your wishes for organ donation are contained in your Will or in your Advance Health Care Directive, you may revoke the donation by amending your Advance Directive or making an amendment to your Will (known as a *Codicil*).

If you want to revoke or amend a donation made on your driver's license, you should follow the instructions provided at the time you completed the organ donation card. If you have any doubts about the status of a driver's license donation, contact your state department of motor vehicles.

The following is a worksheet that you may use to state your health care plan. It allows you to specify your wishes to be followed by health care providers and others who are providing care for you. Note that this worksheet is not a substitute for a Health Care Power of Attorney, wherein you designate someone to make health care decisions on your behalf. (This is discussed further in Chapter 15.)

RECORDING YOUR PLANS
FOR ADVANCE HEALTH CARE PLANNING

An advance health care plan states your wishes for medical care. It is a guide for others who may need to make decisions on your behalf. Be aware that the decisions that you make can always be changed. Further, you can entirely disregard any previously made health care plans by destroying this document. However, if you have provided copies of this form to anyone, you will need to notify them of any changes or of the destruction of this form.

WORKSHEET

1. If I were dying, I would request the following approach to treatment. (If I chose more than one, I have shown the order of preference.)

❑ My main wish would be for care that allows me to be comfortable, peaceful, and free from pain (including hospice care if possible).

❑ I would want to go to the hospital for some treatment if needed for comfort, but I would not want to be connected to life support machines.

❑ If it were unclear whether a life support treatment would improve my chances of living, I would like to have a brief period of treatment in the hospital, but would like the treatment stopped if I did not improve.

❑ I would like life support treatments to prolong my life as long as possible, even if those treatments made me uncomfortable.

❑ I would like to donate organs or tissues and would like life support treatments if needed for organ donation.

❑ Other _____

_____

2. If I were dying and were unable to eat, I would want the following treatments.

❑ I would want to have a tube inserted into my stomach, nose, or mouth to feed me if I could not eat.

❑ I would not want a feeding tube if I could not eat.

3. Following my death, I would want to be an organ, eye, and/or tissue donor.
Yes _____ No _____

4. When I am dying, please keep me as comfortable as possible. Here are some guidelines. (Check the items below that express your wishes. Make notes to personalize these items as you wish.)

❑ Please give me adequate medication to relieve pain, shortness of breath, or other distressing symptoms.

❑ I prefer that enough pain medication be given to me to keep me comfortable, even if this means I am not fully aware of what is going on.

❑ I prefer that I be medicated for pain, but also I want to be aware of my surroundings and what is going on. I understand this may mean my pain control may not be complete.

❑ I wish to have other non-medicine measures taken to help me be comfortable.

❑ Please provide all measures to keep me fresh and clean (baths or sponging, regular mouth care, other personal hygiene, clean linens, back rubs, massage, healing touch, turning, repositioning, and so on).

5. The following will also bring me peace and comfort.

❑ Music (specify type) _____

❑ Readings (specify) _____

❑ Prayers (specify) _____

6. In addition to my family, I wish to have the support of the following person(s).

_____

_____

7. I do not wish to be visited by the following person(s).

_____

_____

Dated: _____

_____

PRINT YOUR NAME

_____

SIGN YOUR NAME

CHAPTER 4:
THE ROLE
OF HOSPICE

The most difficult end-of-life decision to make is acknowledging that there is no longer any chance of living. When all medical options have been exhausted, part of planning for the inevitable includes choosing professional care that will help you during this time.

History of Hospice Care

The term *hospice* can be traced back to medieval times, when it referred to a place of shelter and rest for weary or ill travelers on a long journey. Physician Dame Cicely Saunders founded the first modern hospice, St. Christopher's Hospice, in a residential suburb of London. Saunders introduced the idea of care for the dying to the United States during a 1963 visit to Yale University. Her lecture, given to medical students, nurses, social workers, and chaplains about the concept of hospice care, included photos of terminally ill cancer patients and their families, showing the dramatic differences before and after the symptom control care.

What Hospice Care Is

Considered to be the model for quality, compassionate care for people facing a life-limiting illness or injury, hospice care involves a team-oriented approach. It provides expert medical care, pain management, and emotional and spiritual support, expressly tailored to a patient's needs and wishes. Support is available for your loved ones as well. At the center of hospice care is the belief that each of us has the right to die pain-free and with dignity, and that our families must receive the necessary support to allow us to do so.

Hospice focuses on caring—not curing—and in most cases, care is provided in the patient's home. Hospice care may also be provided in hospice centers, hospitals, nursing homes, and other long-term care facilities. Hospice care is a philosophy of care that accepts dying as a natural part of life. When death is inevitable, hospice seeks neither to hasten nor postpone it.

Ben's Story

My mother-in-law entered the hospital complaining about severe back pain. A biopsy confirmed that she had liver cancer and that it had metastasized to other organs. Her doctors told us that she was terminal and presented us with the option of transferring her to a nursing home or sending her home. A social worker was called in, who provided information about hospice care. With the help of hospice, we brought her to our home, where she was kept comfortable and her pain was managed with medication. Amazingly, although she had become weakened from the biopsy procedure, she managed enough strength to enjoy my son's chocolate birthday cake. Two days later she passed away, surrounded by her family.

How Hospice Care Works

Typically, a family member serves as the primary caregiver, and when appropriate, helps make decisions for the terminally ill individual. Members of the hospice staff make regular visits to the home to assess the patient and provide additional care or other services. Hospice staff is on call twenty-four hours a day, seven days a week. The hospice team develops a care plan that meets each patient's individual needs for pain management and symptom control. The team usually consists of:

➤ the patient's personal physician;

➤ a hospice physician or medical director;

➤ nurses;

➤ home health aides;

➤ social workers;

> clergy or other counselors;
> trained volunteers; and,
> speech, physical, and occupational therapists, if needed.

Services Provided by Hospice Care

Hospice workers provide various medical, emotional, and therapeutic services. Some of the major responsibilities of the hospice team include:

> managing the patient's pain and symptoms;
> assisting the patient with the emotional, psychosocial, and spiritual aspects of dying;
> providing needed drugs, medical supplies, and equipment;
> coaching the family on how to care for the patient;
> delivering special services, such as speech and physical therapy, when needed;
> making short-term inpatient care available when pain or symptoms become too difficult to manage at home; and,
> providing bereavement care and counseling to surviving family and friends.

Qualifying for Hospice Care

Hospice services are available to patients of any age, religion, race, or illness. Hospice care is covered under Medicare, Medicaid, most private insurance plans, HMOs, and other managed care organizations.

Hospice care is for any person who has a life-threatening or terminal illness, including cancer and non-cancer illnesses. To be eligible, your doctor must provide a statement that your life expectancy is six months or less if the illness runs its normal course.

It is a common belief that a person must have a physical disease or disorder to be diagnosed as terminal. However, Medicare has expanded the definition of eligibility requirements to now include the diagnosis of *failure to thrive*. In such cases, the patient has mentally given up his or her will to live and stops eating.

Frank's Story

Frank always took very good care of himself, watching what he ate and exercising regularly. Other then complaints of arthritis, he had no physical problems and was not taking any medication. Shortly after his 92nd birthday, he announced to his wife that walking was

continued

becoming more difficult, which she attributed to his arthritis. However, as each day passed, he spent more time in bed, began losing weight, and started eating smaller meals. His family tried to intervene—to no avail. He refused showering or any other type of hygiene. To the family's surprise, his doctor diagnosed Frank with failure to thrive and told them that he was eligible for hospice care. The family at first fought the idea that Frank was dying, but after a few weeks, it became apparent that it was his wish to die on his terms. Less than two months after hospice care was implemented, Frank passed away.

Affording Hospice Care

Eighty percent of people who use hospice care are over the age of 65, and are entitled to the services offered by their Medicare hospice benefit. This benefit covers virtually all aspects of hospice care with little out-of-pocket expense to the patient or family. As a result, the financial burdens usually associated with caring for a terminally ill patient are virtually nonexistent. In addition, most private health plans and Medicaid in forty-five states and the District of Columbia cover hospice services.

PRACTICAL POINT

If you are under age 65, qualify for Social Security disability, have a terminal illness, and are also receiving Medicare, you qualify for hospice through the Medicare hospice benefits.

CHAPTER 5:
THE FUNERAL SERVICE

Too often, life ends suddenly, leaving the surviving family guessing what would have been their loved one's wishes for a funeral. If you could eavesdrop in a home following a tragedy, you might hear the following conversation.

Would Dad have wanted a simple service at the graveside or a funeral in the church? He was a private person and resisted public attention.

Should we keep the service to just the immediate family? We don't want to insult anyone who would have wanted to attend.

Dad was in the military. He never said, but would he want to be buried in the veterans' cemetery?

Even though Dad remarried, he was married to our mom for fifty years. Isn't it only right that Dad be buried next to Mom?

Would Dad have wanted a closed casket?

A discussion of your funeral and burial should be part of what you do to put your affairs in order. Your loved ones have enough decisions to make after your passing. Whether you put your wishes in writing or simply say them to your family, this type of planning will help them as they endure the difficult time adjusting to your passing.

The Service

In planning your funeral service, you must first decide whether you are comfortable with knowing that spoken words about you may fill a chapel or cemetery. Perhaps you do not want people to fuss about you now and certainly do not want people to do so after you are gone. If that is the case, you must make it known to your loved ones that you want your service to be simple.

You should make your wishes known as to whether you want a service at a house of worship, the funeral home, or the cemetery. Depending on your religious convictions, you should also make known whether to engage clergy to officiate.

Give consideration to whether you want to limit attendance to only your immediate family and closest friends. If it is your wish to keep the number of people small, do not worry about hurting anyone's feelings. People will understand. Also, make your wishes known to your family regarding an open or closed casket.

Ellen's Story

My friend's wife passed away. Ellen was a beautiful lady, but after two years of battling breast cancer, the chemotherapy and radiation had stripped her of her elegance. Ellen's husband decided on an open casket, but despite the wig and makeup, the person lying in the coffin was not the woman we knew and remembered. My wife commented on how Ellen would be so embarrassed for her friends to see her this way. Remember, unless you communicate your wishes, no one will ever know.

You should also decide the type of attire you would like worn to the service. Out of respect, it is commonplace for men to wear jackets and ties, and for women to wear skirts or dresses, when attending a service. However, if you absolutely hate the idea of a tie around your neck, or cannot stand the idea of having to wear a dress, you may want to leave instructions that the attire may be casual. Local customs may also enter into your decisions about attire. For example, in Hawaii, it is common to read the phrase *aloha attire requested* following obituary notices. Aloha attire means it is requested that Hawaiian shirts be worn.

Pallbearers

A casket is designed to be carried by six pallbearers, as this will achieve the optimal weight distribution. In choosing the six people, it is typical to select men. The average weight of a casket is 125 pounds. Add the average weight of a male (175 pounds) or female (140 pounds), and collectively they are lifting 265 to 300 pounds. This is not to say that women cannot be asked to be pallbearers, but most women would prefer not to be asked.

In choosing the six designees, it is recommended that you choose those who are best physically able to perform the task, as you would not want to call upon someone who has a health issue, but would feel ashamed to decline.

Speakers

Most people want a service that allows family and friends the opportunity to share thoughts. Just as it is an honor to be asked to be a pallbearer, it is an honor to be chosen as a speaker.

Your selection of one or more speakers should be based on the speaker's ability to communicate with listeners, as he or she will set the tone of the service. Once you have decided who should speak, you should let that person know of your wishes. He or she may then want to ask you a few questions that will help in his or her preparation.

PRACTICAL POINT

The speaker does not have to be the greatest orator, but should be a good storyteller. He or she should be someone who can meld descriptive words that create your image in the minds of the listeners. Also, since funeral services are emotional, your choice of speaker should be someone who can maintain composure under extreme conditions.

There are no rules for what should be the content of the speech. The speech does not have to be solemn, but it should be dignified. The appropriate use of levity is often welcomed at such highly emotional times. A speaker should not emulate Jay Leno doing his nightly monologue, but the message can maintain dignity with a combination of anecdotes and humor. Remember, it is offensive to the survivors if someone gets up and makes a mockery of the service.

Bernard's Story

A few years back, I attended a graveside service for my friend's grandfather. Bernard had been a widower for many years. In his late eighties, he had begun seeing a lady comparable in age to him. Bernard's great-grandson, who was asked to speak at the service, thought this was the perfect time to try out his Viagra jokes about Grandpa and the girlfriend. This was not the time for such antics.

You may want more of a direct input into the writing of the speech that will be delivered. If this is your desire, you should provide enough information so that the speaker can deliver a retrospective look at your life and how your passing has touched others. A funeral service planner on which you can jot your notes appears on pages 33–35.

FUNERAL SERVICE PLANNER

> Tell your survivors that you filled out this planner. If you do not want to discuss its contents, make sure to inform your loved ones where it may be located.

YOUR NAME: _____

1. FUNERAL HOME

I would like the following funeral home to handle my final wishes.

Name: _____

Phone Number: _____

Address: _____

2. CASKET

Use this space to describe the type of casket (material, color, etc.) you would like. If you already have a model in mind, say so here. This space can also be used to tell your family about the funeral home of your choice and your wishes for the amount of money you would like to spend. Be as descriptive as you would like.

_____

_____

_____

_____

Open _____ or Closed _____ Casket

3. SERVICE

I would like a service: _____ Yes _____ No

If yes, I want a traditional burial service: _____ Yes _____ No

If so, I would like it held at:

House of Worship (insert name) _____

Chapel or Funeral Home (insert name) _____

Graveside Only _____

If I selected something other than graveside only, I would like a graveside service as well: _____ Yes _____ No

4. TYPE OF SERVICE

Religious _____   Personalized _____   Military _____

I would like a memorial service: _____ Yes _____ No

I would like a viewing or visitation: _____ Yes _____ No

5. FLOWERS

The following are the types of flowers I would like at my service.

_____

_____

6. STATIONERY

I would like the following stationery available at my service (i.e., memorial cards, thank you cards, prayer cards).

_____

7. MUSIC

I would like the following music to be played.

    During visitation: _____

    During the service: _____

    Hymns for the service: _____

    Soloist: _____

8. PALLBEARERS

1. _____

2. _____

3. _____

4. _____

5. _____

6. _____

7. _____ (as an alternate)

8. _____ (as an alternate)

9. _____ (as an alternate)

9. CLERGY

I would like the following person to officiate my service.

_____

10. CEMETERY/FINAL RESTING PLACE

If you have already purchased a plot or a space has been reserved for you in a family plot, please enter that information here. If you have not made pre-need arrangements, but have a place in mind, add your wishes here.

_____

_____

_____

11. EULOGY/SPEAKERS

I would like the following person/persons to speak at my service.

_____

_____

_____

12. MONUMENTS

Use this area to describe the type of monument or headstone you would like. If you have already decided on the inscription, provide that information.

_____

_____

_____

13. MISCELLANEOUS

Use this space to add anything that is not covered in this planner.

_____

_____

_____

_____

_____

Writing Your Own Eulogy

Traditionally, a funeral or memorial service includes remarks from family and friends. The family usually chooses the person who knew the decedent the best to deliver the eulogy. However, it is not uncommon to write your own eulogy.

Darlene's Story

My first reaction to a client who raised the idea of writing her own eulogy was one of surprise. I thought Darlene was pompous, controlling, and truly in need of having the last word. Maybe she feared there would not be anyone willing to say something nice about her.

However, upon subsequent meetings in my office, I learned how important it was that those who came to pay tribute remember her exact words. Darlene had been a high school English teacher for over thirty-five years. She reminisced on how her students often marveled at her ability to choose expressive phrases to convey a thought. She inspired many of her students to go on to successful careers in communication and journalism with her powerful writing. Darlene knew that when she passed many of her former students would attend her funeral, and she wanted her message to be heard as if she were still teaching.

The word *eulogy* means "kind or good wishes." Generally, eulogies contain only the most flattering comments about the recently departed, but a eulogy can also be an introspective look at how the deceased met the challenges of life and succeeded. Who knows you better than yourself?

In drafting your own eulogy, the words you choose should be unique to you. Do you have a trademark gesture or a favorite expression? If so, incorporate it to personalize the message. Whether your eulogy describes the obstacles you had to overcome or the successes you enjoyed, people hearing your words will leave the service with those sounds resonating in their minds forever. It is your last opportunity to connect with your loved ones. Unlike an obituary, which is factual (see Chapter 7), your eulogy should define who you are, for all time.

PRACTICAL POINT
Remember that this book is designed to assist in planning for the inevitable. You do not have to be dying to write your eulogy.

After writing your eulogy, carefully choose the person who will deliver your remarks. That person should be someone who shares your passion and will not only speak your words but will express them using your mannerisms and inflection. As an example, Darlene the English teacher chose a fellow teacher in her department to deliver her eulogy. She told her colleague of her choice, but left the eulogy remarks with her Executor in a sealed envelope, which included information about how to get in contact with her colleague.

Your chosen words should not include any remarks that could be interpreted as slanderous. By law, if a remark is made about another, even in jest, the person whom the remark was directed at could sue the estate if it can be proven that he or she suffered financial harm because of the remark. Therefore, do not assume that all those attending your service are invited guests. Except for closed services, almost all houses of worship and funeral homes are open to the public. Therefore, anyone who wants to pay his or her last respects may attend. Your estate could face financial exposure if someone commences legal action and wins.

When you sit down to write your own eulogy, use the following tips to help get you started. You can use the space provided after the tips to jot down some of your initial thoughts.

➤ *What do you want to say?* First, collect the facts—age, family information (including children and marriages), places lived, and career information. Next, think about how you want to be remembered. What personal stories come to mind? What kinds of stories or quotes capture your mind?

➤ *Decide on a theme.* A theme gives purpose to the eulogy, and helps your audience see an overall pattern of behavior and what your life stood for. For example, if you have always been told that you are a great storyteller, mention some of the most fascinating events in your life.

➤ *Organize your notes into a speech.* Begin by organizing your thoughts by segments. Then, weave the segments together into sentences.

➤ *Write your speech for the person you have chosen to deliver the eulogy.* Write out a first draft, sticking closely to the outline you have developed. Fill in any gaps by putting in information to link the topics, making each idea flow into the next. Try to incorporate real life experiences or anecdotes, using bits of humor and light-heartedness, if appropriate. As you write the eulogy, keep the person who you intend to deliver the speech in mind. That person may have certain mannerisms when he or she speaks. Therefore, you may want to adopt this style when writing.

Use the following lines to brainstorm some ideas for your eulogy.

_____

_____

_____

_____

_____

_____

_____

_____

_____

_____

_____

_____

_____

_____

_____

_____

_____

_____

_____

_____

_____

_____

A Celebration of Life Service

Whether your service is graveside or in a chapel, you want your wishes respected. You are also providing this information for your loved ones in order to avoid some of the emotional and difficult decisions that must be made.

However, many people do not want to miss their farewell party. These detail-oriented people want to attend their own Celebration of Life Service.

Celebration of Life Services first became popular in the 1990s. When AIDS was taking so many lives from those who were in their prime, some people chose to plan their own service and attend it. By organizing your own Celebration of Life, it provides you and your loved ones an opportunity to celebrate your life together.

Roger's Story

An affluent client of mine came into my office to update his Trust. Roger informed me that he had been diagnosed with an incurable cancer, and his doctors had given him just sixty days to live. Roger loved to tell stories, throw extravagant parties, and sing. I was not surprised when he handed me an invitation to his Celebration of Life Service. He had rented out a private room in a very swank restaurant and hired a DJ. At the gathering, we celebrated his life, exchanging stories and toasting with his favorite wines. He also sang his favorite song, Frank Sinatra's "My Way." A week later, he passed on. It was his last hurrah and he did it his way.

CHAPTER 6:
PREPLANNING ARRANGEMENTS

As mentioned in Chapter 5, your discussion with family members regarding funeral arrangements can provide opportunities for your loved ones to know your personal preferences, feelings, and desires. In the event of your death, knowing that they are carrying out your wishes will comfort your family. This is especially significant if someone desires a simple, inexpensive funeral or no funeral at all. In the grieving period following the death of a loved one, family members can easily overextend themselves financially on funeral arrangements. If they know you definitely wanted a simple funeral, then the family will not feel guilty about spending less.

Take time to collect information on varying costs, and calmly choose funeral arrangements and final interment ahead of time. In this way, you can carefully choose the specific items you want and need, and can compare prices offered by one or more funeral providers. By considering all the options available now, you eliminate the possibility of your family making hasty and often expensive decisions under sales pressure at the funeral home.

Pre-Need Arrangements

Though more common in Europe and other parts of the world where the subject of planning for one's own passing is not taboo, many people are now electing to make pre-need arrangements for their funeral and final interment.

This may include arranging and paying for a funeral home for the services, selecting a casket, and purchasing a grave. This advance planning removes the emotional decisions that your loved ones would have to make.

Pre-need arrangement does not necessarily have to be accompanied by prepayment of funeral goods and services. The following is a brief outline of the potential arguments for prepayment.

➤ Prepayment allows for a feeling of security that prearrangements will be carried out.

➤ It provides peace of mind to those who have no relatives or other person to handle funeral arrangements.

➤ Prepayment protects survivors from making uncomfortable or emotional decisions under the stress of bereavement.

➤ You can do comparison shopping among competing funeral providers.

➤ You reduce the risk that survivors will incur large expenses at the time of need.

There are also arguments to be made against prepayment, such as the following.

➤ There is no guarantee that the funeral home will be in business at the time of your passing.

➤ If you move, you may not be able to shift the arrangements to another location or receive a refund.

➤ In many states, money deposited in a pre-need account receives little or no accrued interest.

➤ In some states, monies paid do not have to be placed in trust, in which case, the recipient of the funds may be free to spend the funds.

➤ Your survivors may not even be aware that funeral expenses have been prepaid.

Alternatives to Prepayment

As an alternative to prepayment, you may wish to consider setting up a specific interest-bearing bank account that your family can use to pay for services at the time of need. Your family will benefit from the interest the account will accrue, and will be protected if the funeral home goes out of business.

A Totten Trust is an example of a special type of savings account, to which the depositor adds the name of a beneficiary. The beneficiary, who can be a funeral home, friend, or relative, is trusted to use the funds as the depositor directs. The advantage of a Totten Trust is that the funds stay in your control, and can be withdrawn in an emergency or transferred if you should move to a new area. It is revocable during your lifetime, but in most states, becomes irrevocable at the time of death.

Burial Insurance

Like a special savings account, a standard life insurance (or burial insurance) policy can be taken out to cover anticipated funeral expenses. Upon death, the policy can provide the funds needed to cover funeral expenses.

> PRACTICAL POINT
>
> Prepayment arrangements with funeral homes should be considered only if the funds are adequately safeguarded (placed in trust), if the funeral home has a sound reputation, if you are certain that you will want to use the services of this particular funeral home, and if the price is guaranteed. Regardless, you should consult with an attorney before signing any agreement. If you do make such arrangements, be sure to attach the agreement with the funeral home to your Funeral Planner. (see Chapter 5.)

Funeral Homes and the Funeral Rule

Most decisions about purchasing funeral goods and services are made by people when they are grieving and under time constraints. Thinking ahead may help you make informed and thoughtful decisions about funeral arrangements. In this way, you can carefully choose the specific items you want and need, and can compare prices offered by one or more funeral providers.

The Federal Trade Commission (FTC) has developed a trade regulation rule concerning funeral industry practices. It is called the *Funeral Rule*, and its purpose is to enable consumers to obtain information about funeral arrangements.

The Funeral Rule was enacted to make it easier for you to select only those products and services you want or need, and to pay for only those you select. When you inquire in person about funeral arrangements, the funeral home will give you a written price list that outlines all goods and services available. When arranging a funeral, you can purchase individual items, or buy an entire package of goods and services. If you want to purchase a casket, the funeral provider will supply a list that describes all the available selections and their prices. Regardless, you should call or visit at least two funeral homes and cemeteries to compare prices, so that you can more accurately assess the total costs.

What is on the Price List?

Funerals can be basic or extravagant. A basic funeral generally includes the costs of:

➢ moving the body to the funeral home;
➢ using the funeral home facilities;
➢ embalming, providing cosmetology and restoration, and dressing the body;
➢ purchasing the coffin;
➢ using the hearse;
➢ arranging for pallbearers;
➢ providing a guest register and acknowledgment cards;
➢ paying professional service fees;
➢ obtaining burial and transit permits;
➢ placing newspaper death notices; and,
➢ filing the death certificate.

All of the above goods and services are generally included in a package-priced traditional funeral. The following costs are usually additional, depending on the type of service selected:

➢ clergy's honorarium;
➢ music;
➢ limousines;
➢ flowers;
➢ burial clothes;
➢ cremation service charges;
➢ urn;
➢ marker or monument;
➢ crypt;
➢ cemetery charges for opening and closing the grave;

> burial plot;
> cemetery perpetual care charges; and,
> burial vault or grave liner.

Caskets

A casket is the single most expensive item in a traditional funeral. Traditionally, caskets were sold only by funeral homes, but now they may be purchased at cemeteries and Internet sites. Available in many styles and prices, caskets may be made from metal, wood, fiberglass, or plastic.

The basic cost of a casket is between $500 and $1,500, and funeral homes may mark up the price by as much as 300%. Under the Funeral Rule, a funeral home cannot charge extra if you provide your own casket from an outside source.

NOTE: A casket is not required for direct cremation, immediate burial, or donation of the body to science.

In addition, most cemeteries require the use of a grave liner or vault. These outer burial containers surround the casket in the grave to prevent the ground from sinking as settling occurs over time. In some states, both funeral homes and cemeteries sell vaults and liners.

Embalming

The Funeral Rule requires funeral providers to give consumers information about embalming that can help them decide whether to purchase this service. Under the Rule, a funeral provider must disclose in writing that:
> except in certain special cases, embalming is not required by law;
> you usually have the right to choose cremation or immediate burial if you do not want embalming;
> certain funeral arrangements, such as a funeral with a viewing, may make embalming a practical necessity, and thus, a required purchase; and,
> the embalming process is not reversible.

As ridiculous as this last disclosure may sound, there was a case where a family requested embalming for their loved one and then had a change of mind. When the funeral home advised the family that the embalming process had taken place and that there was nothing that could be done to reverse it, the family sued. To protect themselves from future suits, members of the funeral industry now make this part of their disclosures.

Funeral Homes

The following are commonly asked questions of funeral home directors. Remember, do not be intimidated. You have the right to be informed and should not hesitate to ask questions such as the following.

- ➤ Can I have your general price list, casket price list, and outer burial container price list?
- ➤ Is your funeral home independently owned and operated, or is it part of a funeral home chain?
- ➤ What is the basic fee for a funeral?
- ➤ What is the fee for *immediate burial* (burial without embalming, and no service or viewing)?
- ➤ Does this fee include transferring the body to the funeral home?
- ➤ What is your fee for washing and disinfecting?
- ➤ Is there a fee for body preparation and makeup? If so, what is your fee?
- ➤ What is the charge to open the grave at the cemetery? Is a burial container necessary at that cemetery, and if so, what is the cost of a basic cement liner?

Problems with the Funeral Home

If you or your family has a problem with the funeral home, first attempt to resolve it with the funeral director. If the problem is not resolved, you should contact the licensing board that regulates funeral homes in your state or the following organizations.

International Conference of Funeral Service Examining Boards
1885 Shelby Lane
Fayetteville, AR 72704
479-442-7076
www.cfseb.org

Funeral Service Consumer Assistance Program
P.O. Box 486
Elk Grove, WI 53122
800-662-7666

Cremation

Generally less expensive than a traditional burial, cremation is a process in which the body is placed in an inexpensive container and taken to the crematory, where it is placed in a retort, exposed to intense heat, and reduced to ashes. The ashes (or remains) may then be stored in an urn or other receptacle, or disposed of by the survivors.

The costs may include the cremation itself, transportation of the body and cremated remains, an urn or other container for the ashes, burial in a niche in a columbarium (a special building designed to hold cremation urns) or in a burial plot, a memorialization plaque, and scattering of the ashes (unless done personally).

In terms of what material to use for storage, a suitable container, such as one made of cardboard, knock-down-wood, pressboard, or fiberboard is usually all that is required by law.

PRACTICAL POINT
State and local laws should be checked before disposing of ashes, as states and localities have regulations restricting the process of scattering cremated remains over land or water.

Burial or Cremation—Make Your Wishes Known

Your Last Will and Testament may not be read for weeks after the funeral and burial has occurred. This is because the family is emotionally distraught and cannot contemplate dealing with any legal requirements that they perceive the Will may include. However, a Will often states one's wishes for final interment. As a result, many times children pay for the funeral and burial only to discover that Dad's Will stated that he wished to be cremated. The simple solution to prevent this from happening is to have a conversation with your loved ones.

In drafting a Will, you can state your wishes regarding final interment. For religious reasons, some people prefer a certain type of cemetery for burial. A person who has served in the military is entitled to be buried in a veterans' cemetery. Accordingly, whether your wishes are burial or cremation, it is important that your loved ones know of your decision. Have this discussion with your children, no matter how uncomfortable it might seem. Perhaps when you are out for dinner, bring up the conversation. Even if the kids respond, "we don't want to hear about it or talk about it," just say it once. They will remember your wishes. That is all it takes. Then, finish your dinner.

Cemeteries

Funeral arrangements are only part of the expense if you choose burial in a cemetery or entombment in a mausoleum. Cemetery costs generally include:

➢ a burial plot or mausoleum crypt;

➢ opening and closing the grave (which can be more expensive on weekends);

➢ a vault or a less expensive grave liner (although not required by law, one may be required by individual cemeteries to prevent subsequent collapse of the grave); and,

➢ a memorial (marker, monument, or plaque).

The location of the plot and the use of materials for markers or stones have a direct effect on the cost. Most cemeteries require that a plot be paid for in full before it is used.

Veteran Funerals

If you are a veteran, the U.S. Department of Veterans Affairs provides for a small burial allowance for burial in a private cemetery. In addition, all veterans can receive a burial flag and burial in a national cemetery at no charge. For the location of the closest national cemetery, call 800-827-1000 and ask for the Veterans Affairs (VA) office for your region. Graves in VA national cemeteries cannot be reserved in advance. However, reservations made prior to 1962 will be honored. If burial will be in a private cemetery and you desire a government headstone or marker, request and complete VA Form 40-1330 (Application for Standard Government Headstone or Marker for Installation in a Private or State Veteran's Cemetery) in advance, and place it with your veteran's military discharge papers for use at the time of need. Be sure to advise your family that this has been done.

Memorial Societies

There are over two hundred memorial societies throughout the United States and Canada. Volunteers run these nonprofit organizations, which were established to provide consumers with choices in making funeral arrangements outside of the pressure of a funeral home. Memorial societies generally do not offer merchandise or funeral services. Instead, they have entered into arrangements with cooperating funeral providers to take care of the needs of their members.

Membership in a memorial society is obtained by paying a one-time membership fee of $15 to $25. If a member dies while away from his or her society's area, the memorial society at or close to the place of death can provide assistance. A complete listing of funeral societies can be found on the Internet at **www.funerals.org** by clicking on the link "Directory of Nonprofit Funeral Consumer Groups" or by calling 800-765-0107.

Headstone Inscriptions

Your wishes as to the style of the memorial marker and the inscription on the stone may be part of planning for the inevitable. As more people are making pre-need arrangements that include grave plot purchases, it is becoming common to make known your wishes for the inscription on the stone.

Why does it matter how your memorial marker reads? If you have walked through a cemetery, there are markers that include simply the name and year of birth and death. However, leaving a few memory thoughts or expressions that conjure up the mental image of you would be most appreciated by your loved ones.

Audrey's Story

In my first year of practice, I was given Audrey's case. She was suing her brother over the inscription that he chose for their mother's headstone. Mom was buried in Pennsylvania, though both siblings lived in California. A year after the funeral, Audrey went back East and visited her mom's grave. She was horrified that her brother chose to remember their mother with the words, "mother, teacher, and practical jokester."

If you made an impact with your life, whether by serving in the military, excelling in your profession, making others laugh, or being the best Nana to your grandchildren, your loved ones who visit your grave will come to revisit their memories of you. That special memory thought that you choose to be inscribed on the stone will help inspire their visit.

Some suggestions you may want to consider include the following inscriptions.

- ➤ *Gone, but not forgotten*
- ➤ *Entered into rest*
- ➤ *Until we meet again*
- ➤ *Forever in our hearts*
- ➤ *At rest with God*
- ➤ *Rest in Peace*
- ➤ *Too well loved to ever be forgotten*
- ➤ *The song is ended, but the melody lingers on*
- ➤ *Sweetly sleeping*
- ➤ *Loving memories lasting forever*
- ➤ *Not lost to memory! Not lost to love! But gone to our Father's house above*
- ➤ *Step softly, a dream lies buried here*
- ➤ *Your love will light my way, your memory will ever be with me*
- ➤ *What we keep in memory is ours unchanged forever*
- ➤ *Death is only a shadow across the path to heaven*
- ➤ *At the going down of the sun, and in the morning we will remember them*

In selecting memorial stones, you may wish to have a conversation with your spouse and your family about the stone to be placed, and about whether to have a family marker that can accommodate the names of both spouses.

PRACTICAL POINT

As gruesome as it may sound, cemeteries will bury two persons in the same grave. The first person is buried nine feet below the surface and the second person is buried six feet under. Upon the passing of the second person, the cemetery will charge an additional fee to reopen the grave. Therefore, if this is something that you wish to consider, you should make your wishes known. Again, it is one little step in removing the emotional decisions that your loved ones would have to eventually make.

Second Marriages

Suppose you had a long-term marriage and your spouse died. You subsequently remarried and are now ill. Do you want to be buried with your first or present spouse? This can be a very sensitive subject to address with your spouse. However, this book talks about planning for the inevitable and respecting your wishes. Have the conversation and make your wishes known. You will feel better that you did.

CHAPTER 7:
OBITUARIES AND VIDEO LETTERS

Upon a loved one's passing, a funeral home director will offer to place a notice or obituary in the newspaper. If the family is so inclined, the funeral director will obtain statistical information, including the date of birth and death, place of birth, and the names of surviving family members. Newspapers charge according to the size of the obituary. As part of their services, funeral homes coordinate with newspapers to arrange for publication. If your wishes are to not have an obituary published, you should make this known to your family.

However, if you would like more than a statistical summary of your life published, the following sample is offered to assist you in preparing the information.

SAMPLE OBITUARY

Lockhart, Margaret
Newport Beach, California—January 1, 2006

Margaret was born October 12, 1937. She was the daughter of Lewis A. and Rebecca (Smith) Brewster. Margaret is survived by two children, Michael Lockhart of Bayport, Virginia, and Sheryl Adams of Long Beach, New York; a brother, Joseph Brewster, of Rochester, New York; a sister, Kim Riley, of Portofino, Italy; and several grandchildren, nieces, and nephews. She was predeceased by her parents; a sister, Emily; and her husband, James.

Margaret was a speech pathologist and retired from the Emerson Institute of Speech and Hearing Development in 1994. She was also a member of the National Guild for the Blind, a volunteer for Meals on Wheels, and a past president of the Greater Audubon Society of Newport Beach.

Friends may call at The Betterman Funeral Chapel, 123 Main Street, Newport Beach, on Monday, January 3 from 2 p.m. to 4 p.m. and 7 p.m. to 9 p.m. The funeral service will be at 10:00 a.m. Tuesday, January 4 at the funeral home. Burial will be at Mt. Hope Cemetery. In lieu of flowers, donations can be sent to the Audubon Society of Newport Beach.

NOTE: Of course, the date of death and the paragraph about the funeral would be completed at a later time.

Obituaries can be written at the time of death or before. Many people find it helpful to write their own obituary notice in advance for the following reasons.

➤ The surviving family members may not remember or may struggle to remember specific dates (birth, employment, retirement, previous deaths).

➤ The surviving family members may not know proper spellings of people's names, places, companies, or organizations.

➤ The surviving family members may not know all of the deceased's memberships in volunteer organizations.

➤ The self-written obituary could specify a favorite charity for donations that the surviving family would not have considered.

An obituary notice does not have to be limited to only statistical information. Many obituaries include sections taken from the person's eulogy, as well as quotes from favorite books, poems, and movies. Obituary notices may also include photos.

It is important that you make known to your survivors that you have written an obituary. The following is a worksheet for completing your obituary.

OBITUARY WORKSHEET

YOUR FULL LEGAL NAME *(nickname may be included in parentheses)*

_____

CITY OR TOWN OF RESIDENCE _____

DATE OF BIRTH _____

PLACE OF BIRTH _____

SURVIVED BY LIST *(Insert names of living relatives)*

Spouse _____

Parents _____

_____

Children _____

_____

Sisters _____

_____

Brothers _____

_____

Grandchildren and Great-Grandchildren (insert numbers of) _____

Predeceased by (spouse, child, parent, sibling) _____

_____

EDUCATION/DEGREES

_____

_____

WORK HISTORY

_____

_____

OPTIONAL INFORMATION *(special interests or hobbies)*

_____

_____

ASSOCIATIONS *(membership in local or national organizations)*

_____

_____

SPECIAL AFFILIATIONS/VOLUNTEER WORK

_____

_____

MILITARY SERVICE

_____

_____

OTHER

_____

_____

Video Letters

Unlike most obituaries, which provide statistical information, a video letter allows you to express your feelings and thoughts. It is not to be confused with a video will, as you are not discussing what property you are leaving and to whom. Instead, when you make a video letter, you create a lasting image of who you are, where you came from, and what message you want to leave.

> PRACTICAL POINT
>
> Video letters are not substitutes for written Wills. The law requires that a Will must be signed, dated, witnessed, and sometimes notarized to be valid.

Video letters first gained popularity during the Gulf War in 1991. As American troops were sent to the Middle East, many troops left behind video messages to their children and families. This was an opportunity for children to see and hear the parent who might never come back.

Sylvia's Story

A client of mine, literally on her deathbed, called my office about leaving a video message. I arranged for a video production service to go to Sylvia's home and tape her. For days she had been under heavy sedation, but somehow, on this day, she mustered the strength to speak what were almost her last words. Sylvia was a single parent of a beautiful daughter who was almost three. Sylvia wanted to leave a message for her little girl that she could replay as often as she liked. Hours after the taping, Sylvia passed away peacefully, but her message lives on forever.

CHAPTER 8:
IF YOU HAVE TO RELOCATE

People have to relocate for many reasons. Your present residence may be too large for you to maintain, or your health may no longer allow you to climb stairs. Perhaps you are having difficulty with day-to-day activities, such as dressing and bathing, and you have considered moving into an assisted living residence where help is available.

Housing options generally fall into five categories, and are based on the level of services required.

1. *Independent living retirement communities.* These are hotel-like settings designed for seniors who are independent, but want meals, housekeeping, activities, transportation, and security provided.

2. *Assisted living facilities.* These facilities provide the same services as independent living retirement communities. In addition, residents receive assistance in taking their medications, bathing, grooming, and dressing.

3. *Nursing homes.* If you are disabled and you require daily nursing care as well as other support services, nursing homes provide comprehensive care services in a single setting.

4. *Board and care.* These facilities are private residences converted to accommodate up to six residents. These residences are typically owned and managed by people with nursing backgrounds.

5. *Group homes.* Group homes are private homes in which residents divide the cost of rent, housekeeping services, utilities, and meals. The residents are independent and do not need assistance in their daily needs.

Depending on your physical abilities, assisted living residences offer comfortable living arrangements. Typically, they are furnished, one-room apartments that are part of a large senior living complex. You can usually bring some of your own furniture, and facilities accommodate both couples and individuals. Meals are provided in a main dining room. The homes provide daily activities, and van transportation is available to take you shopping and to your doctor appointments. Further, if your medical condition should worsen, many assisted living facilities are associated with long-term care residences.

Another type of residence that is gaining popularity is the board and care home. Unlike assisted living residences, where hundreds of seniors may reside, board and care homes are converted single-family residences that now accommodate up to six residents. Again, each resident has his or her own bedroom, and the residents eat their meals together in the dining room. The home is staffed twenty-four hours a day by nurses and other trained medical providers. Transportation to doctor appointments is provided.

Making the Decision

Often, a person who lives alone agonizes over making a decision to relocate. Even when there is immediate family to live with, you may not want to become a burden on your children. It is important that you make your decision collectively with your family, as they have concerns that must be addressed. Regardless, it is best to make a decision to relocate on your terms and not force your children to make a decision for you.

Over the years, I have received dozens of calls from children of clients. The conversation always begins the same: "Dad can no longer live in his house alone. It's not safe. We want to move him into an assisted living home, but he won't hear of it. Can we get a court order to make him move?"

My advice comes down to whether the parent is competent to make his or her own decisions. Assuming he or she is, a court will not order someone to move. Regardless, if the children are raising concerns, it is probably time for you and your entire family to sit down and talk about your future living needs. Visiting facilities may help set aside any misconceptions you have about assisted living residences. It is important to note that moving into an assisted living facility does not signal that you are relinquishing any freedoms or independence. It does mean that you recognize that you may, at times, need assistance with daily activities.

Regardless of your financial or physical condition, it can be very emotional to leave your home of many years. One elderly client faced with this dilemma asked how she could walk away from the home that provided so many wonderful memories. As she said, "If these walls could talk, it would fill hundreds of pages of books." In response to my clients' concerns, I often suggest that they take pictures of the home and walls in each room. Then, collect your memory thoughts in writing as a lasting memory for your children, grandchildren, and generations to come.

Frances's Story

One client was kind enough to give me a copy of her memory thoughts. Her letter follows.

"This letter is written to my grandchildren, who I so dearly love. As Poppa and I embark on this new journey, I am filled with excitement and sorrow. Our home has been the centerpiece for so many wonderful occasions. I thought you would like it if I shared my thoughts with you.

This past summer, my daughter and her family, who reside in California, traveled back to the home she grew up in as we prepared for our move to California. What I thought would be a hurried weekend evolved into a rare 72-hour snapshot of mine and Poppa's lives. With family and friends, we reminisced about our fifty years of living in the home and community we so cherished and loved. From this experience, I learned both how fragile a lifetime is and the importance of family and the loving relationships we make during our lifetime.

When thinking about our moving to California, I never truly realized how much we would be leaving behind. I suppose I always thought of our home as "Nana and Poppa's," the typical grandparents' home that was filled with love to spoil and dote on our

continued

grandchildren. Until today, I had never comprehended how much we were giving up in this move. It was truly the move of a lifetime.

It's no wonder the house in which our family was raised sold quickly. Every room was neatly arranged. My fine china was elegantly displayed through the glass doors of the dining room cabinet. The many family photos adorned every wall and table, and my kids' rooms remain unchanged with the same double beds that the boys shared. My daughter wanted her room painted pink, but I am sure the new owners will want to change the color. All in all, for fifty years this has been our home, and I am sure the new owners should enjoy many wonderful years as we have.

But as exciting as was the anticipated move to southern California, there was also sadness in the air. We were not only leaving our home of fifty years, but were saying good-bye to a lifetime.

On this hot, humid summer morning, my neighbor, Henrietta (everyone calls her Henny), came by to talk to my daughter and me. There was polite conversation that Henny would visit; that she would spend time in California to escape the brutally cold winters of the northeast. There would be a guestroom for her if she would like. But we knew it was only talk.

That weekend we also drove to Brooklyn to see Poppa's sister, Jenny. Jenny turned 90 only a few months ago. Poppa's eyes welled up as his sister was wheeled into the room. Their eyes met and her face opened with a charming smile. Poppa was nervous; his usual Jay Leno-style monologue was noticeably missing. He was at a loss for words as his eyes examined her tired body. Could this have been his big sister who had raised him from the age of 12 after their mother died?

For one hour Jenny and my Poppa laughed and cried. They reminisced about a lifetime; not only about the weddings and grandchildren, but the very difficult Depression years when food was so scarce. The ironic part of aging is that often the mind can remember details from many years ago, but cannot recall yesterday.

Then, all of a sudden, there was no conversation. What Poppa wanted to say was good-bye, but his lips would not move. Would he ever see Aunt Jenny again? He clutched her small body as her hand patted the side of his face. Her hands began to tremble as he rose to his feet and said, "I love you, everything will be all right."

And then, like a receiving line at a wedding, we passed Jenny, hugging and kissing good-bye.

Poppa continued to cry as the elevator descended to the first floor. "That's my sister, how can I leave?" We had no answer, but I remember Allison saying, "Poppa, Aunt Jenny loves you." Poppa reached out for her hand and held her tight.

The weekend continued with nonstop waves of neighbors and good friends whose bonds of friendship were cemented years ago. There were the cordial expressions of "good luck" and "stay in touch." But I sensed mixed feelings of envy and sadness; sadness because a good friend was leaving and envy because they were left behind. Would we ever meet again? Is this one more page in the book of life? For many of the elderly, time is all we have. And thinking about time can be so cruel.

The movers arrived on Monday morning, and within hours the house of fifty years was no longer recognizable. The walls were stripped of all the family photos and community awards. All that remained of the furniture were the impressions in the carpeting.

Finally, it was time to leave. We gathered for one more picture in front of the house, and then walked away. I can no longer go "back home" but my mind is filled with beautiful memories to last a lifetime.

Prior to this weekend, I never thought that so many people loved Poppa and me as much as they did. I also never realized that we had touched so many lives.

My lifetime experience has taught me that happiness is nurtured in the home and becomes a valuable resource tool to influence future success. Above all, I have learned the importance of having roots. Feeling a connection to where I am from will help in guiding me to where I am now going."

Reprinted with permission from Frances Schieren, who passed away peacefully at the age of 81, seven years after her move to California. At the time of her passing, she was surrounded by her husband, children, and grandchildren.

As I mentioned earlier, any decision to relocate is best if you have been involved in the decision process. However, if it can be proven that you are not competent to make your own decisions, a court could be asked to appoint a conservator for you. (see Chapter 15.) Typically, a family member will petition the court and cite specific reasons why it is not in your best interest to live alone. Your doctor or some other medical provider who has reviewed your medical records usually supports this petition. The court, before granting the request, will often employ its own medical professional to examine your medical records and personally evaluate you, and then make a recommendation to the court. If the petition is granted, you no longer have the ability to make your own decisions as to where to live.

Children, because they do not always live in close proximity with their parents, often find out that the parents are not acting competently after the fact. When I am asked to represent children of a parent who allegedly is no longer competent, the process can be emotionally grinding for all involved. To illustrate, my client's father was slowly giving away his estate to strangers. Apparently, anyone could ring his doorbell and ask for money, and he would hand over a check. He was also not bathing, changing his clothes, or remembering to take his medicine. His son asked me to petition for him to be conservator of his dad. After a brief hearing, the request was granted.

There are numerous Internet sites available that provide information about relocation and senior living options that may be available in your community. You can also contact your state's department of health services for referral information.

In addition, if you need assistance in moving and your needs are greater than what a traditional moving company provides, there are businesses that specialize in organizing your home for the move, moving your property, and then setting up your new residence. This removes the stress often associated with moving. One company that offers these services is Helping Hands. Their website is **www.helpinghands-online.com**.

CHAPTER 9:
IF YOU ARE ALONE

None of us have a crystal ball to look into and see when our time is up. We all know of stories where tragedy strikes suddenly, with no warning. That is why it is so important to have a plan in place regardless of your present health condition.

Planning for the inevitable typically includes discussing your plans for when you are no longer here with loved ones. However, your situation may be one in which you have no surviving family members or people to whom you feel close enough to act on your behalf. This chapter will assist you in having an orderly plan in place.

Medical Care

If you have not executed an Advance Health Care Power of Attorney appointing someone to act on your behalf to make medical decisions, you should still sign a Living Will. This document represents your wishes for or against artificial life support if you become terminally ill. You are not selecting anyone to act for you. The document only requires your signature, and must be witnessed or notarized. Make sure that your doctor is given a copy of the Living Will for placement in your chart. See Chapter 14 for more information on Living Wills.

In addition, to prepare for the possibility of your medical condition reaching a point where you are unable to think clearly and make decisions for yourself, you should have a conversation with your doctor and other health care professionals who are providing care for you. If you express your wishes, they will be noted in your record.

Hospice

As discussed in Chapter 4, your medical condition may meet the requirements of hospice care if you have private health insurance, qualify for Medicare, and are either receiving Social Security or Social Security disability benefits. Hospice is a program that provides for home health care. Under hospice, your medications and other health aids (wheelchair, bathroom commode, hospital bed) are provided. Other benefits include nursing care and assistance with daily activities, such as dressing and feeding.

If your medical condition would be best addressed in a hospital setting, there are hospice facilities where you can receive inpatient care.

Home Nursing and Caregiver Services

There are employment agencies that specialize in placing caregivers in your home to assist you. A phone directory or Internet search under the category "senior care" will produce a listing of agencies in your community.

After you are asked a few questions, the agency will schedule a time to have one of its social workers come out to your home to more fully evaluate your needs. To illustrate, a person who needs assistance with food shopping and home cleaning, but can dress and bathe him- or herself, has fewer demands than a person who cannot go to the bathroom without help.

The skilled level of care that you require will determine the cost of employment. Nursing care provided by a registered nurse will be more expensive than a caregiver who can assist you with your personal needs, but cannot dispense medication.

Depending on your budget and needs, home health care providers may either *live in* based on a daily rate, or *live out* and receive hourly pay. Regardless, make sure that you ask the agency to produce references that you can verify. Also, only work with an agency that can provide an insurance bond. That way, in the event that a worker is hurt in your home, there is insurance coverage. Ask the agency for replacement guarantees in the event the person it places in your home does not work out.

Estate Planning

Chapter 13 discusses whether or not you need a Will or a Trust. If you do have assets, such as real property or investment accounts, and there is no one you wish to leave property to, you may wish to write a Will leaving your property to specifically named charities. Because a Will requires you appoint someone to be the Executor of the estate, you may wish to consider asking a member of your clergy or someone that you can trust. If you are leaving your estate to a charity, contact the charity so that the people there are aware of your bequest. In addition, national charities have programs in place where they also act as the Executor.

> PRACTICAL POINT
> Do not ask a bank or other financial institution to serve as your Executor. Such entities, in addition to any statutory fees that they are entitled to through probate, typically will tack on administrative expenses. As a result, your intended gift is often greatly diminished in value.

If you do not have any monetary assets that you wish to leave to designated persons or charities, and your estate does not require a formal Will or Trust, you may still want to make a list of your personal property with instructions for disposition. What you may think is of little or no value may have value to someone else. Organizations like Goodwill can make arrangements to pick up furniture and clothing. Your local library is a good place to donate your books.

If you have pets, Chapter 12 provides information for making arrangements for the care of your pets when you are no longer here. Your pets have provided uncompromising love to you. The worst scenario for an animal would be for its owner to pass away and leave the animal locked in the home with no food or water, until someone discovers the newspapers piling up on the lawn and calls the police.

Stuart's Story

Several years ago, a very nice gentleman came into my office to make a Will. Stuart had never married and lived alone. During the consultation, he informed me that he was diagnosed with an inoperable brain tumor. Five months earlier, the doctors had told him that he probably would not survive six months. He was apparently not a very social person and had no friends, though he did exchange hellos with his neighbor now and then. Stuart informed the neighbor of his condition and asked if she would call me if he should die. I asked how the neighbor would know when he passed away. He said he always fell asleep with the television on and would turn it off when he woke up the next morning. If the neighbor heard the TV still playing late in the morning, she was to call the police. Two weeks after Stuart signed his documents, he died peacefully in his sleep.

Final Interment

It is becoming more and more popular to make pre-need arrangements with funeral homes. All details can be arranged prior to the event of your passing. See Chapter 6 for more information.

Organ Donation

If you carry a donor card, it will provide instructions for organ donation upon your passing. You can further specify your wishes in a Living Will. Organ donation is discussed more fully in Chapter 3.

CHAPTER 10:
HOW TO BEHAVE

The most disappointing calls I receive are from siblings who are bickering with each other over their parents' estate. This can be a stressful time for anyone who has lost a loved one. Having a conversation with your children while you are still here might avoid or at least minimize potential problems that could arise after you have passed. The following guidelines discuss potential issues and can serve as a primer from a parent to their children on how to behave with their siblings after the parent is gone.

Your Choice of Executor and Trustee

Children sometimes feel slighted when one child is chosen over another to be their parents' Executor or Trustee. Children wonder if their parents did not consider them smart enough or otherwise suitable for the job.

Your choice for Executor, Trustee, or any Power of Attorney is typically decided based on practicalities and not favoritism. Perhaps your oldest child lives out of state, and therefore, it would not be logical for him or her to handle the financial decisions that would have to be made when you are no longer here. Having a conversation with your children after you have completed your estate planning paperwork will go a long way to avoid future problems between your children.

Division of Money and Other Liquid Assets

In the great majority of Wills and Trusts, there is usually an equal division of assets among children. However, you may have very good reasons not to divide your estate equally. Perhaps you have a child with whom you had little or no contact for many years, and you may feel that this child does not deserve an equal distribution. You may have one child who has been down on his or her luck, while your other child has done very well financially and is self-sufficient. You may want to give more to the child who really needs the money. Talking with your children about your decision might help them understand your reasons and avoid resentment later.

Bruce's Story

I prepared a Trust for a widower. Bruce's daughter and her child lived with him in his house. He had an older daughter who was married to a very successful businessman. The daughter who lived with him took care of Bruce, especially when he became ill. She had very little income and Bruce decided to leave his house, which was his major asset, to her. Upon his passing, the older daughter offered to have a collation for friends and family after the funeral service at her house, since it could accommodate more people. Weeks later, after the Trust was read and she realized that she was not left an interest in the home, she sent her younger sister an itemized bill for paper plates, plastic utensils, deli meats, mustard, and mayonnaise as her share of the cost for the collation. A very caustic note accompanied the bill. When the younger sister did not pay, she was sued in small claims court. Fortunately, the older sister lost, but had Bruce discussed his reasons for distributing his estate the way he did with his children, it may have saved the sisters' relationship.

If a conversation is not possible, leave a sealed letter, addressed to each child, and instruct that it is only to be delivered upon your passing. In your letter, you can explain your decisions. Be careful, however, if you have omitted a child from your Will. Unless your Will names your child and then specifically disinherits him or her, most courts will allow that child to challenge the Will for not being included in your estate. See Chapter 13 for a further discussion on omitted heirs.

Division of Personal Property

A Will or Trust often does not specify what each child is left. Instead, the language often reads, "All my personal property to be divided equally between my children." In this case, you should advise your children before you pass that they should respect each other's wishes in deciding upon a fair distribution.

Renee's Story

Renee had three daughters. She was afraid that after her passing, the daughters would tear each other apart in an effort to take as much as possible from the house for themselves. In an effort to prevent this fighting, Renee appointed the Public Guardian as the Executor of her Will. The Public Guardian is a court-appointed official who steps in to secure the premises after an individual's death. The Public Guardian of Renee's estate had instructions to padlock the home and then change the locks. Thereafter, he was to auction off all of the contents, deduct his administrative fee, and divide the proceeds among the three daughters.

Division of Personal Property Without a Will

As discussed in Chapter 13, not everyone needs a Will. However, you probably have some specific items of personal property that you wish to leave to your children. Whether it is a coin collection, jewelry, or other family heirloom, you would like your children to enjoy it after you are no longer here. In such cases, tell your children what is left for them. Make sure each child knows what the others are to receive. That way, there are no surprises.

Jewelry

Jewelry is the one item that often creates the most fighting between children, especially when there are no specific instructions left. The sons usually have no interest, but the daughters and daughters-in-law are ready to run a marathon to collect the gold. Make it perfectly clear to your children and in-laws what jewelry they are to receive. Be aware, however, that even with these precautions in place, jewelry often mysteriously disappears after one's passing.

Julia's Story

Julia's mother always told her that all of her jewelry would become Julia's. However, just to avoid the possibility that some of the jewelry would disappear by the time Julia flew across the country for the funeral, her mother told her that all of the expensive jewelry was kept in a coffee can on the second shelf of the refrigerator. That way, in case there were some daughters-in-law with sticky fingers, they would be foiled trying to pull off the heist. Sure enough, when Julia arrived, one of the daughters-in-law approached her and said, "Didn't Mom have a set of pearl earrings? I didn't see them when I was picking out clothes for the funeral."

Let's Be Friends

One's passing often results in either bringing families closer together or driving them further apart. If siblings were close before, they will become closer. However, if there was jealousy or animosity, whether there was reason for it or not, some siblings view the loss of a parent as the perfect time to finally cut themselves off from any future family ties.

Parents are often tuned into ongoing disputes between their children, even when the children are not aware of what the parent knows. If you know of sibling disputes, convey to your children how important it is to you that they bury the hatchet and live their lives as a family. Remind them that friends may be gone tomorrow, but family is for life.

Ethel's Story

Ethel had two daughters who had not talked to each other for over ten years. It was Ethel's dying wish that her children make peace. She said she could not die until that happened. As death was imminent, she pleaded with her daughters to speak with each other. Her doctors were amazed at how she clung to life. Barely able to speak, her body wracked with pain, she acknowledged me with her eyes when I visited her in the hospice facility. I told her that I received a call from her daughter in Chicago who was on her way to see her. That night, both daughters appeared in her room, having made peace. Ethel passed away that night.

Your Behavior Towards Others

It would be the greatest understatement to say that learning that you may no longer be here is stressful. Many books have been authored by grief counselors and other health care professionals advising how one should accept the news and respond. That all sounds great—unless the news concerns you. No one can tell you how you feel or how you will feel. No one can suggest or dictate your emotions when you are facing the greatest challenge of your life. It is understandable that you will be angry, moody, unfriendly, or all of these things and more. Still, for whatever it is worth, consider the following.

> ➤ This is not the time to be mean, rude, or ungrateful to your family and friends. Your family and friends are your support group. If they are sincerely offering to help, take their offer.

> ➤ Do not make unreasonable demands on others. Be sensitive to the schedules of your family and friends.

> ➤ It is not only about you. End-of-life decisions involve you and all those who surround you. Remember, it is your survivors who need to be strong to continue after you are gone.

> ➤ Conduct yourself in the way you want to be remembered. We are all judged after we are gone, and faults tend to be recalled first.

> ➤ Have tolerance. Do not criticize or question the motives of others unless you have proof that the person has acted insincerely. Wait to hear the explanation before you make assumptions that could lead to hurt feelings.

> ➤ Be receptive to health care professionals. This is their job and they signed on to help you. By making their job easier, you will be helping yourself.

> ➤ Live each day. Whatever time is remaining, be as physically and mentally productive as you can.

Tim's Story

Tim was appointed trustee of his uncle's estate. His uncle, Louis, had no children with his wife of forty-five years. Louis and Louann were living alone in their home and refused to go into an assisted living residence. They had always had a reputation in the family for being mean and ornery, but Tim could never have predicted what was to come.

continued

Over a period of two years, Tim made twenty-nine trips to Las Vegas from Los Angeles. In addition to buying groceries, paying bills, and scheduling and keeping doctor appointments, Tim had the stressful and time-consuming responsibility of trying to keep the home health care providers from leaving. This is because Louis and Louann were verbally abusive to each other and to the health care workers. Out of spite, if Louann liked one aide, Louis would purposely despise her. They would also shove and throw food that was prepared for them, not allow the aides to change the bed sheets, and resist all attempts at showering. Other family members tried to visit, but were refused entrance. Over the two-year period, more than one-hundred health care workers were employed in the home. Tim eventually went through every senior aide agency in Las Vegas.

One day, the latest health care worker called Tim and said that Louis was refusing to eat. He was also less agitated. Less than ten days later, Louis passed away, followed after seven weeks by Louann. Predictably, as the extended family gathered for the funerals, tales of rudeness overshadowed stories of kindness and fond memories. How sad!

CHAPTER 11:
LEGACY WILLS

By planning for the inevitable, you are putting your legal and financial affairs in proper order. This may include estate planning and financial arrangements. All this is done for the benefit of your survivors. Likewise, preparing for the inevitable should include writing a Legacy Will.

Chapter 13 discusses Wills that state to whom property will go upon a person's passing. In contrast, Legacy Wills pass one's values, ideas, and personal reflections to family members and other loved ones. They can include descriptions of significant events from one's lifetime.

A Legacy Will has been described as a love letter to your family. Every Legacy Will is as unique as the person writing it. It is one of the most coveted and meaningful gifts you can leave to your family and friends. You do not have to have a large estate or any property to write a Legacy Will. Instead, your gift of words will live on in the hearts and minds of your family and friends forever.

The length of a Legacy Will is inconsequential. What you choose to include in your Legacy Will helps determine the length of the document. Writing your Legacy Will does not need to be a time-consuming undertaking. Instead, a few caring and perhaps thought-provoking paragraphs are all that is needed to express your legacy. Regardless of your writing skills, it is your message that will live on in the hearts of your readers.

Writing Your Legacy Will

There is no textbook that describes how to write a Legacy Will. Just remember that you are unique. What you have learned during your lifetime, your thoughts, experiences, and feelings may be passed on to your loved ones through your chosen words, and will become your legacy. Some suggested topics and common themes for a Legacy Will include:

> ➤ your beliefs and opinions;
> ➤ things you did to act on your values;
> ➤ something you learned from your spouse, grandparents, parents, siblings, or children;
> ➤ life's lessons;
> ➤ your happiest and funniest moments;
> ➤ why you love your family and will miss them;
> ➤ your favorite job;
> ➤ your favorite television show, movie, play, music, or book;
> ➤ your good and bad habits;
> ➤ your hopes for future generations;
> ➤ spiritual values important to you;
> ➤ something you learned from experience;
> ➤ your political beliefs and positions on issues;
> ➤ something you are grateful for;
> ➤ your hopes for the future;
> ➤ important events in your life;
> ➤ what you regret not having done; and,
> ➤ forgiving others and asking for forgiveness.

In writing your Legacy Will, be very careful in choosing your written words. It should not be used as your soapbox for making unkind and disparaging statements about someone. If the intended target of your remarks believes them to be libelous, your estate could be held legally liable for damages. Therefore, the best advice is to bite your tongue and focus on the positive messages you want to leave behind.

The Legacy Will on the next page is reprinted with the permission of one of my clients. You may wish to use this as a reference in drafting your own. Use page 76 to jot down notes for your own Legacy Will.

SAMPLE LEGACY WILL

To my wonderful children,

You know how much family has always meant to me. Thank you for making my life so complete. I love each and every one of you. We have always supported each other as a family. My wish is for each of you to accomplish something in life that you can leave to others; that will become your legacy. Follow your dreams and never give up.

In my life with Dad, we have definitely endured both the good times as well as the bad. But we were strong and weathered the storm. I hope you can learn from our experiences in raising your children. Remember, though at times our decision may not have seemed right, we always had your best interests at heart.

You have given me four beautiful grandchildren. What a wonderful gift. And you are raising your children to be loving, kind, and giving. Remember each day when you look into their faces that their eyes are a window into the future. Nurture that future, as they are our leaders for tomorrow.

I also want to express my love for Ed and Denise. From the day you became part of our family, I never thought of you as son-in-law or daughter-in-law, but as my son and daughter.

Please read this letter to my beautiful grandchildren when they are old enough to understand that Grandma left a special message for them. To Sarah, Amy, Samuel, and David, you have given Grandma so much love and joy. I will miss you terribly, but want you to know that when you close your eyes to go to sleep at night, I am there with you. I will always protect you.

Finally, my last wish to you is that you will try to be closer to your dad. This will be a very difficult time for him. He needs to know you are always there without his asking. Dad is a very private man and often doesn't say what he feels. I guess you learn these things about a person when you have lived with them for as many years as we have. Please take care of Dad.

I love you forever and ever.

Mom

CHAPTER 12:
DISPOSING OF PERSONAL PROPERTY AND CLEANING HOUSE

Making arrangements for disposing of a loved one's clothing and other personal effects is one of the hardest tasks a survivor must do, as it represents closure. It is a physical reminder that a loved one is no longer here.

An important step for you to take in preparing for the inevitable is to exercise prudence when discarding papers. Pay close attention to any papers that have your Social Security number or credit card numbers on them. Because identity theft has become a serious issue, you may want to invest in a paper shredder before hauling files out to the trash.

PRACTICAL POINT
The IRS may question information on a tax return for three years after it was filed, and it has six years to audit your returns for unreported income. Accordingly, tax preparers and accountants recommend that tax returns and supporting documentation be kept for at least seven years.

Disposing of Embarrassing Items

In the movie *About Schmidt*, Jack Nicholson portrays a husband coming to grips with the sudden death of his wife. Shortly after the funeral, and after the family and friends have returned home, Nicholson finds himself staring at his wife's clothing hanging in the bedroom closet. As he begins to box the contents of the closet, he discovers a stack of envelopes wrapped in a bow. To his surprise and dismay, the envelopes contain love letters exchanged between his wife and her boyfriend. All of a sudden, his marriage of more than forty-five years seemed invalidated. The woman he thought he knew so well had a secret past.

Buried within the shoe boxes of cancelled checks and receipts for appliances that broke years ago, there may be papers you do not want anyone to see. Likewise, the discovery by your family of an embarrassing photo could tarnish your reputation, as you are no longer here to defend yourself.

Sarah and Nicole's Story

Sarah and Nicole contacted me. Their mom had passed away two years ago and their dad nine months later. The family home was being sold, and in preparation, the sisters were boxing up mementos they wanted to keep. Upon opening one of the cabinet doors of their father's workbench, they discovered a box that contained numerous photos of their dad with a woman they immediately recognized as his secretary. The photos were taken in Las Vegas, New Orleans, San Francisco, and other cities he had traveled to on business. The sisters were so upset by their discovery that they were seeking my advice to have their father's grave exhumed and relocated to another part of the cemetery, so that their mother would no longer share a grave with her husband.

The phrase "I will take it to my grave" is usually said in defiance of a person who is trying to gain information from you, but you may have reasons to have never revealed to others some event or relationship. Therefore, it is good advice to take inventory of all of your personal effects so that something damaging does not surface later.

Keeping Promises to Leave Property

A properly drafted Will outlines what specific items of personal property are to be left and to whom. It is not uncommon, however, to tell someone during your lifetime that you want to leave a specific item of property to him or her. The problem may occur when there is a misunderstanding between family members as to who was left what.

To prevent such misunderstandings, you should leave a note (handwritten or typed) that includes the names of recipients and descriptions of the specific items of property you wish to leave. This note is known as a *holographic codicil*. You must sign and date the note, and fasten it to the Will. However, the note is *not* to be witnessed or notarized, or it will invalidate the codicil. This recommendation is intended only to apply to items of personal property, such as jewelry and other mementos, and not cash distributions.

Distributing Personal Property During Your Lifetime

You may choose to make distributions of your property during your lifetime so that you can enjoy the gift of giving. This, of course, ensures that the intended recipient of the gift receives the gift and removes the responsibility of your Executor to deliver the gift.

If you choose to do so, review and update your Will to make sure that any item you give away during your lifetime is not still listed in your Will. This prevents a later challenge by a recipient from claiming that an item left for him or her in the Will was never received.

My cousins in Phoenix have come up with a solution to determine what items of personal property their children really want, and it removes any guessing on my cousins' part. They have informed their kids that prior to relocating to an assisted living residence, the kids may come to their home and take whatever they want. By the end of the weekend, whatever is still there will go to Goodwill.

Making Charitable Donations of Your Property

In planning for the inevitable, do not assume that your survivors will want your personal effects. In fact, disposal of personal property often becomes a burden for your loved ones. This is not to say that Dad's lucky fishing rod or Mom's favorite Pyrex casserole dish will not have sentimental value, but the reality is that most items will be disposed of through garage sales, or offered to Goodwill and other charities.

By taking inventory of your property, you may find that there are specific items you wish to donate to a charity. Most charities will come to your home and pick up the merchandise. This applies to all items, including vehicles. Also, you can make arrangements for the items to be picked up after notification of your passing. You may prefer this option, for example, so you can still use your car. By searching the Internet for car donations, you will find many companies that will arrange to have your vehicle picked up, whether it is operable or not. You can also select the name of the charity that you wish to donate the proceeds to.

Mildred's Story

One of the most heartbreaking comments I ever heard was from a client talking to me about her personal effects. Mildred was a widow and never had children. She also had no surviving relatives, and was leaving her entire estate to several charities. As for her personal property, Mildred told me that she had an extensive collection of porcelain picture frames, but she had left instructions with her trustee to remove and discard all the pictures before delivering the frames to Goodwill. She commented that after she was gone, there would be no one left to enjoy looking at the photos.

Frequent Flyer Miles

If you have accumulated frequent flyer miles, you should inquire with the mileage program about donating your miles to a specified charity. Depending on the airline and the number of miles that you have in your account, miles may be donated in your name.

Don't Be a Pack Rat

Putting your affairs in order extends to neatly organizing and arranging your home. Your survivors, who will be involved in the transition process, must contend with the difficult realization that you are no longer here. This is especially the case if you lived alone, as your loved ones are now faced with the tasks of removing pictures from the walls, emptying closets of your clothes, and disposing of the personal items that once represented you.

In doing so, your family and friends will greatly appreciate it if you would remove any obstacles that could be dangerous to their health. Leaving dust-covered boxes of clutter to trip over only makes their job more difficult. The following is a checklist to help you organize your surroundings.

Checklist for Organizing Your Home

○ **Take inventory of your clothing.** If you have not worn it in the last decade, chances are you will never wear it again. Bring it to Goodwill or take it to some other charity.

○ **Go through your files of cancelled checks, bank statements, and receipts for purchases and paid invoices.** Unless advised otherwise by your accountant, you can destroy records that are more than seven years old.

○ **Put photos and news clippings in albums or marked boxes.** Do not leave loose photos lying around.

○ **Throw out all those magazines, catalogs, and other useless articles of papers that have been piling up.** Only keep them if you are saving them for a specific reason (such as leaving them for someone). It is one less thing for your family to have to haul away.

○ **Clean out the kitchen cabinets and drawers.** You do not need those outdated food coupons, takeout menus of restaurants that have long closed, and warranties for appliances that broke years ago.

○ **Eyeball each room in your residence.** Throw out that broken chair in the corner, the dead plant from the kitchen, and pens that don't work.

Caring for Your Pets

Finally, make arrangements for your pets. Many people feel deeply for their pets, but the law views them as property. As such, they should be provided for in preparation of the inevitable.

Dogs and cats are creatures of habit. Any break in their daily routine can cause disorientation. Accordingly, a plan should be in place for your pets, whether you live alone or not.

It seems once a year there is always a story on the news about neighbors who complain about a foul smell coming from an apartment. Once the police enter, they discover a person who has passed away. Upon further inspection, they find a cat or dog that has not been fed for days hiding in the corner. The animal is seriously malnourished and scared.

In choosing who will care for your pet, it is only logical to select someone who would give your pet the same love that you have provided. Hopefully, that person can also provide a similar living environment for your pet. Remember, though pets do adapt to change, a golden retriever who is used to the run of the backyard may have a hard time spending its days cooped up in a one-bedroom apartment.

Once a choice for your pet is made, you should inform that person to make sure he or she will accept. That person should also be provided with all health information about your pet, along with the name of the veterinarian. If you wish to make specific provisions for your pets, including monetary amounts to provide for their care, such provisions should be in your Will. (See the "Will Provisions for your Pets" section in Chapter 13.)

If you have exhausted names of people to care for your animal, there are many organizations that accept animals for adoption, including the American Society for the Prevention of Cruelty to Animals (ASPCA). You can contact ASPCA at 212-876-7700 or **www.aspca.org**. In addition, the pet store chain PetSmart has a very active program for placing animals for adoption. You can contact PetSmart at 800-738-1385 ext. 2518 or **www.petsmart.com**.

CHAPTER 13:
WILLS
AND TRUSTS

By planning for the inevitable, you are taking the first steps in protecting the future lives of your loved ones when you are no longer here. It is prudent to be prepared to help avoid the disruption that is often faced by your survivors upon your passing. Depending on your situation, it is important to have an understanding of the legal consequences of your passing. Though not everyone may need a Will or a Trust, a consultation with an attorney will help you decide whether or not you require some type of estate planning. If you do not create a Will or Trust, you run the risk of leaving a final and lasting impression on your loved ones that you did not care enough about them to spare them the confusion, hassle, and unnecessary expenses that could have all been avoided with proper planning.

Last Wills and Testaments

There is a general misconception as to what a Will does. In simplest terms, a Will is a letter of instructions for the person you appoint to carry out your last wishes. Your wishes may describe how you want your property to be divided, including specific bequests naming the individuals or charities to receive your property. However, depending on state law, your estate may still have to be probated if the value of your assets exceeds a certain limit.

PRACTICAL POINT

Even if you have no property to distribute, your Will can express your wishes regarding final interment. If it is your wish to be cremated, your Will should state that desire. Likewise, if, for religious reasons, you wish to be buried in a certain type of cemetery, you may include such language in your Will.

When clients first contact my office to make a Will, I mail them the worksheet on pages 87–88, which helps organize their assets and express their wishes for distribution to their heirs. This way, they are prepared for their appointment. You may wish to use this worksheet prior to completing the Will document on pages 89–90. (A Will better suited for people with minor children appears on pages 95–96.)

WILL PREPARATION WORKSHEET

I. YOUR ESTATE

List the contents of your estate, including bank accounts, stocks, 401(k)s, IRAs, real estate, motor vehicles, life insurance, and anything else that you may own, whether by yourself or with another person. For this purpose, an estimate of the value is sufficient.

Bank Accounts

1. _____
2. _____
3. _____
4. _____

Stocks, Bonds, Treasury Notes, Other Investments

1. _____
2. _____
3. _____
4. _____

Life Insurance, IRAs, Pension, 401(k)

1. _____
2. _____
3. _____
4. _____

Real Estate (address)

1. _____
2. _____

Tangible Personal Property
(This category includes furniture, jewelry, and artwork—anything of significant value or that you would like to go to a particular person.)

1. _____
2. _____
3. _____
4. _____

II. BENEFICIARIES

List the people you would like to receive a part of your estate, including family members, friends, and charities. As you transfer this information to your Will in the "Bequests" section, determine what percentage or specific item each person should receive. Typically, you would leave your entire estate to your spouse, except for bequests of specific items to others. If your spouse has predeceased you, divide your estate equally among your children.

Spouse _____

Children

1. _____
2. _____
3. _____
4. _____

continued

Other Individuals

(Include friends, grandchildren, brothers, sisters, or anyone else to whom you would like to give a part of your estate.)

1. _____
2. _____
3. _____
4. _____

Charities

(List any religious or other nonprofit organizations to which you would like to make a bequest. This may reduce the taxes on your estate.)

1. _____
2. _____
3. _____
4. _____

III. EXECUTOR

Name the person or persons you would like to appoint to administer your estate. He or she will carry out your wishes as stated in your will. Also name an alternate in case the first person appointed cannot serve for any reason.

Executor _____

Alternate _____

IV. GUARDIAN OF CHILDREN

The most important purpose of a will for most younger people is the appointment of a guardian for their children under age 18. Also name an alternate in case the first person appointed cannot serve for any reason.

Guardian _____

Alternate _____

After you have filled out the worksheet, add your specific information to the standard Will form on the next two pages.

LAST WILL AND TESTAMENT
OF

_____

I, _____, a resident of _____ County, state of _____, declare this to be my Will and I hereby revoke all Wills and Codicils previously made by me.

FIRST: <u>Family Status:</u>
I declare that I am married to _____ and I have _____ children from this marriage, namely, _____, _____, _____.

SECOND: <u>Appointment of Executor:</u>
I appoint _____ as Executor of this Will, to serve without bond. If the person named shall have predeceased me or should for any reason be unable or unwilling to serve as Executor, I appoint _____ as Executor of this Will, to serve without bond.

THIRD: <u>Executor's Power:</u>
I authorize my Executor to sell, at either public or private sale, any property belonging to my estate, either with or without notice, subject only to such confirmation as may be required by law, and to hold, manage, and operate any such property.

FOURTH: <u>Non-Exercise of Power of Appointment:</u>
I hereby refrain from exercising any testamentary power of appointment that I may have at the time of my death.

FIFTH: <u>Taxes:</u>
My Executor shall pay from the residue of my estate all inheritance, estate, and other death taxes (excluding any additional tax that may be assessed under Internal Revenue Code Section 2032[a], including interest and penalties, that may, because of my death, be attributable to any assets properly inventoried in my probate estate). The taxes shall be charged against my estate as though they were ordinary expenses of administration without adjustment among the beneficiaries of my Will.

SIXTH: <u>Bequests:</u>
I give, devise, and bequeath my entire estate as follows:

   A.

   B.

continued

SEVENTH: <u>Non-Contest:</u>

Except as otherwise provided in this Will, I have intentionally and with full knowledge omitted to provide for heirs. If any beneficiary under this Will in any manner, directly or indirectly, contests this Will or any part of its provisions, any share or interest in my estate given to that contesting beneficiary under this Will is revoked and shall be disposed of in the same manner provided herein as if that contesting beneficiary had predeceased me without issue.

EIGHTH: <u>Definitions:</u>

For the purpose of construing the terms of this Will:

A. Except when the context of this Will requires otherwise, the singular includes the plural, and the masculine gender includes the feminine and neuter.

B. The terms "issue," "child," and "children" include a person born out of wedlock if a parent-child relationship exists between this person and one through whom this person claims benefits under this Will. These terms do not include persons who are adults at the time of adoption.

C. For purposes of this Will, any beneficiary who dies within sixty (60) days after my death shall be deemed to have died before me.

Executed this _____ day of _____, 200_____ at _____,
state of _____.

_____
Name

On this date, _____ signed this document and declared it to be his/her LAST WILL in our presence, and in the presence of each other, signed as witnesses below. Each of us observed the signing of this Will by him/her and by each other subscribing witness and knows that each signature is the true signature of the person whose name was signed.

Each of us is a competent witness. We are acquainted with him/her and attest that he/she is now more than eighteen (18) years of age. To the best of our knowledge, he/she is of sound mind at this time and is not acting under duress, menace, fraud, misrepresentation or undue influence.

Each of us declares under penalty of perjury that the foregoing statement is true and correct, and that each of us signed below on this _____day of _____,
200_____, at _____, state of _____.

Signature: _____

Print Name: _____

Address: _____

_____

Signature: _____

Print Name: _____

Address: _____

_____

Special Will Provisions

Most Wills are very similar in the language used. That is, except for name changes, the language remains the same and the Will simply names beneficiaries and the amount or percentage they are to receive. A Will may also describe specific items of personal property and to whom it is left. Will provisions may also include directions for use of some of the assets immediately upon passing.

Connie's Story

Connie's fondest memories were of the trips she and her husband took with her children to Las Vegas. It had been several years since the last trip and her health was failing. In her Will, Connie allocated a specific amount of money, with instructions for her Executor to take her children and their families to Las Vegas in memory of their mom. She even allocated a set amount for gambling.

Occasionally, you may want a certain event to occur before a beneficiary can inherit property. For example, if you had a son who started college and made several attempts to complete his education, but never succeeded and was now going from to job to job, you may want to include a provision that your son's share of the estate will be held in a trust until he graduates from college and receives a degree. This is usually enough of an incentive to get your child back to school and to get a degree.

However, not all provisions require something positive to occur. A person making a Will may decide to leave a disproportionate amount to an heir because of some past event. Often, when parents are estranged from their children, or have become angered or upset as a result of some event, a parent may write a Will that specifically disinherits a child or leaves a specific amount that is less than the other children's share. To illustrate, if there are four children, but one child has disappointed his or her parents, a Will provision might include language that leaves $1,000 to that child and the remaining assets of the estate to the other three children in equal shares.

> PRACTICAL POINT
>
> Failing to mention your child does not remove his or her inheritance rights. A Will must state that the child is *specifically disinherited*. Even mentioning the child by name and leaving him or her one dollar will not be enough to prevent him or her from challenging the estate. It is wise to consult with an attorney if you are planning to treat one child differently than the others.

Using Negative Language in a Will

Though a Will allows you to describe how you want to divide your estate, it should not be used to praise or condemn someone for his or her prior conduct. As mentioned, an heir can be specifically disinherited by stating, "I specifically disinherit John Smith." Doing so will normally defeat a Will contest by the omitted heir. However, people who draft their own Wills sometimes add language as to why someone was omitted, citing specific reasons. Citing reasons for disinheritance actually gives the disinherited person a stronger case to receive an inheritance than just using the standard language.

George's Story

George wrote his own Will and spent an entire page describing why his son was a failure in his eyes and not deserving of any money from the estate. The son filed a Will contest challenging the language of the Will. During the investigative process, it was discovered that George had been taking medication and was being influenced by others. The son had made several attempts to reconcile with his father. On the eve of the trial, the attorney representing the estate called to settle. Had George retained an attorney to draft the Will inserting the proper disinheritance language, the son's attempt at the Will contest would have been defeated.

Will Provisions for Pets

As discussed in Chapter 12, it is important that you make arrangements for your pets after you are no longer here. This usually refers to who will take care of your pets. However, if you wish to make a specific monetary provision for your pets, it should be spelled out in your Will. For example, a client of mine wanted to make sure that her prized poodle, Sadie, received the best of care after she was gone. The poodle had had some health issues, and my client wanted to provide that money was set aside if her dog needed additional medical care. In her Will, she made a specific provision of $10,000 for Sadie's future medical care.

Frequent Flyer Miles

If you are a frequent flyer and have accumulated miles in a mileage program, you should inquire with the airline to determine their policy about leaving the miles in your Will to a designated person. Some programs allow you to leave them to a spouse, family member, or another specified person. Usually, the airline will require a certified copy of the death certificate, as well as a copy of the Will or Trust that contains the specific bequest. You may wish to donate the miles to a specific charity, as discussed in Chapter 12.

Guardianships

Contrary to common belief, minor children are not automatically placed with grandparents or other relatives upon your and your spouse's passing. Instead, in many states, a relative must first petition the court to be appointed guardian. However, by having a simple Will, the court process can be entirely avoided.

One of the provisions of a Will is called "Appointment of Guardian." This allows you to appoint someone to be the guardian of your minor child upon your (and, if married, your spouse's) passing.

Regardless of whether you have a home or other property that you wish to leave to others, an appointment of guardianship protects your child if you are no longer here. For this reason alone, it is important to have a Will.

If you leave a surviving spouse, there is no issue of guardianship if you do not have a Will, as the surviving spouse is the parent. Still, estate planning is similar to playing a game of chess. In drafting a Will, the goal is to try to calculate for as many moves or events as possible. Therefore, in the event that both you and your spouse were to die together, the guardianship provisions would address the issue of who would raise your child.

In choosing the guardian of your children, it is common to select a relative. Of course, in making your choice, you should consider the financial abilities of the person you choose to raise your child, as well as the quality of life your child will receive. It is also very important that you have a conversation with the person you have selected before drafting the Will.

Stan and Susie's Story

Stan and Susie died in a head-on collision. They had two minor children. Stan had no living parents, Susie's mother was very ill, and all other relatives lived out of state. As required by law, social services were called when the parents died, and unfortunately, the children were placed in two separate foster care homes. It was several weeks before a court hearing was held to approve the petition of the children's uncle for guardianship. Had there been a Will, all of this would have been avoided.

PRACTICAL POINT

When selecting a guardian, do not select both a husband and wife as the guardians, because the couple could divorce. If another relative challenges the guardianship, some courts could conclude that your appointment is not enforceable, because the divorce invalidated your choice of "John and Mary Smith." Instead, select one name, even if that person is married.

If you are divorced, regardless of whether you have shared custody or only visitation, do not assume that your child will go to live with your ex-spouse upon your passing. In most cases, this will occur. However, if there have been issues previously raised between you and your ex concerning his or her ability to raise your child, your choice for guardian could be argued upon your passing as what you believed was in the best interest of your child. As courts decide custody issues in the best interest and welfare of the child, your choice is important.

The following is a Will with a guardian provision (see paragraph 4). If you have minor children, you can this form instead of the Will form found on pages 89–90.

LAST WILL AND TESTAMENT
OF

_____

I, _____, a resident of _____ County, state of _____, declare this to be my Will and I hereby revoke all Wills and Codicils previously made by me.

FIRST: <u>Family Status</u>:
I declare that I am married to _____ and that I have _____ child/children by this marriage namely, _____, _____, and _____.

SECOND: <u>Appointment of Executor</u>:
I appoint _____ as Executor of this Will, to serve without bond. If the person named shall have predeceased me or should for any reason be unable or unwilling to serve as Executor, I appoint _____ as Executor of this Will, to serve without bond.

THIRD: <u>Executor's Power</u>:
I authorize my Executor to sell, at either public or private sale, any property belonging to my estate, either with or without notice, subject only to such confirmation as may be required by law, and to hold, manage, and operate any such property.

FOURTH: <u>Nomination of Guardian</u>:
If my child/children are minors at the time of my death, and my spouse has predeceased me, then I hereby nominate _____ as Guardian of my child/children. If the Guardian named declines or is unable to act, or after appointment ceases to act as Guardian, then I do nominate _____ as Guardian of my child/children.

FIFTH: <u>Non-Exercise of Power of Appointment</u>:
I hereby refrain from exercising any testamentary power of appointment that I may have at the time of my death.

SIXTH: <u>Taxes</u>:
My Executor shall pay from the residue of my estate all inheritance, estate, and other death taxes (excluding any additional tax that may be assessed under Internal Revenue Code Section 2032[a], including interest and penalties, that may, because of my death, be attributable to any assets properly inventoried in my probate estate). The taxes shall be charged against my estate as though they were ordinary expenses of administration without adjustment among the beneficiaries of my Will.

SEVENTH: <u>Bequests</u>:
I give, devise, and bequeath my entire estate as follows:

    A.

    B.

continued

EIGHTH: <u>Non-Contest:</u>

Except as otherwise provided in this Will, I have intentionally and with full knowledge omitted to provide for heirs. If any beneficiary under this Will in any manner, directly or indirectly, contests this Will or any part of its provisions, any share or interest in my estate given to that contesting beneficiary under this Will is revoked and shall be disposed of in the same manner provided herein as if that contesting beneficiary had predeceased me without issue.

NINTH: <u>Definitions:</u>

For the purpose of construing the terms of this Will:

A. Except when the context of this Will requires otherwise, the singular includes the plural, and the masculine gender includes the feminine and neuter.

B. The terms "issue," "child," and "children" include a person born out of wedlock if a parent-child relationship exists between this person and one through whom this person claims benefits under this Will. These terms do not include persons who are adults at the time of adoption.

C. For purposes of this will, any beneficiary who dies within sixty (60) days after my death shall be deemed to have died before me.

Executed this _____ day of _____, 200_____ at _____, state of _____.

_____
Name

On this date, _____ signed this document and declared it to be his/her LAST WILL in our presence, and in the presence of each other, signed as witnesses below. Each of us observed the signing of this Will by him/her and by each other subscribing witness and knows that each signature is the true signature of the person whose name was signed.

Each of us is a competent witness. We are acquainted with him/her and attest that he/she is now more than eighteen (18) years of age. To the best of our knowledge, he/she is of sound mind at this time and is not acting under duress, menace, fraud, misrepresentation or undue influence.

Each of us declares under penalty of perjury that the foregoing statement is true and correct, and that each of us signed below on this _____ day of _____, 200_____, at _____, state of _____.

Signature: _____
Print Name: _____
Address: _____
_____

Signature: _____
Print Name: _____
Address: _____
_____

Same-Sex Relationships

In same-sex relationships where one partner is the biological parent, unless the other partner adopted the child, the child does not by law go to the surviving partner upon the partner's death. Instead, a relative of the child could petition for guardianship. In addition, the surviving partner could lose all rights to visitation. If a Will is in place, the court will consider the last wishes of the biological parent in determining guardianship.

Sue and Mary's Story

Sue and Mary were in a long-term relationship. They wanted to start a family and knew the difficulties encountered by couples trying to adopt. They agreed that Sue would be artificially inseminated. A beautiful baby girl was born. However, Mary did not petition the court to adopt the child, and Sue never signed a Will naming Mary as guardian. Shortly after the girl turned two, Sue was diagnosed with cervical cancer, and despite treatment, died. Almost immediately upon her passing, Sue's parents went to court seeking full custody of their grandchild. The grandparents had legal rights, being the parents of the biological mother. Despite Mary's argument that she was the best person to raise the child, the court sided with the grandparents. Further, as the court concluded that Mary was not related to the child, she was also not entitled to visitation rights. Had Sue named Mary in her Will as guardian of the child, the court would have considered Sue's intention in deciding what was in the best interests of the child.

Providing Health Information

As discussed, it is important to name a guardian for your children. In the event of a tragedy, your guardian will be better prepared to assume care for your children if he or she has access to their health information. Therefore, you should provide your child's health history, doctor's name, and health insurance carrier to a guardian. Following is a health information worksheet that you can use to organize this information.

FAMILY MEDICAL HISTORY AND
HEALTH INSURANCE INFORMATION

Your child's name _____

List any known allergies (food, medicine, other) _____

_____

Physician's name, address, phone number _____

_____

_____

Your child's name _____

List any known allergies (food, medicine, other) _____

_____

Physician's name, address, phone number _____

_____

_____

Your child's name _____

List any known allergies (food, medicine, other) _____

_____

Physician's name, address, phone number _____

_____

_____

Name of health insurance company _____

Policy/group number _____

Claims phone number _____

Location of immunization records _____

Additional information _____

_____

_____

_____

PERSONAL MEDICAL HISTORY

Questions could arise concerning diseases or illnesses that might have a link to family history. This information could be useful should a child or other closely related family member become sick. To pass on your medical history information, a personal health history worksheet should be completed. Following is a sample that you can use, with space at the end to note illnesses or conditions that other family members had.

NAME OF PRIMARY PHYSICIAN:

_____

Phone Number: _____
Address: _____

PLEASE CIRCLE EACH MEDICAL CONDITION THAT YOU HAVE EVER BEEN TREATED FOR:

Alcoholism	High blood pressure
Alzheimer's disease	High cholesterol
Anemia/hemophilia	Kidney disorders
Cancer/leukemia/benign tumors	Lung problems/asthma
Circulatory problems	Mental illness
Crippling arthritis	Muscular disorders/muscular dystrophy/multiple sclerosis
Depression	Nervous disorders/convulsions/seizures
Diabetes—child/adult	Parkinson's disease
Digestive disorders/colitis/ulcers	Stroke
Heart disorders	Vision problems/glaucoma

Other (specify) _____
Other (specify) _____
Other (specify) _____

If you have any known allergies (food, medicine, plant, other), please list them:

_____

_____

Please use these lines to list names of family members who had any of the above conditions, and which conditions they had:

_____

_____

_____

Revocable Trusts versus Wills

The decision whether to make a Last Will and Testament or a Revocable Trust is often determined by the value of your estate. This is because a probate proceeding must be commenced when an estate's value exceeds a certain amount. For example, in California, if the value is greater than $100,000, a probate case must be filed before property can be transferred, regardless of whether there was a Will.

In addition to the probate process being lengthy, the court assesses probate fees, which are payable from the estate. All states have set schedules of probate fees and they are applied on a sliding scale downward. To illustrate, in California, the first $100,000 of value is assessed at 4%. Depending on the law in your state, the value of property may be what is assessed, not the equity you have in it. So, if a home is worth $400,000 and $395,000 is owed on the mortgage, the estate is still assessed at the $400,000 value.

Dennis's Story

Dennis had lived alone for many years. His modest, two-bedroom home was worth less than $200,000. Dennis's mortgage was $140,000. Unfortunately, he developed an online gambling addiction and borrowed $45,000 against his home on an equity line of credit. Although he had a Will leaving the home to his son, there were no other assets in the estate available to pay the probate fees, which exceeded $6,000. Further, Dennis's son was unable to pay the fees or continue to pay the mortgages on the property. As a result, the home was foreclosed and the son lost the property. Had the property been held in a trust, there would have been no probate fees. The property might have still gone into foreclosure, but the son would have had time to sell the home to salvage whatever equity remained.

A revocable trust is set up during your lifetime. You are the *trustor*, or maker of the trust, and the trust includes language as to your wishes for distribution of your assets to your beneficiaries upon your passing. In addition, assets such as your residence and financial accounts are transferred into the trust. This is commonly known as the *pourover provision*, as your assets pour over into the trust.

When there is a *revocable trust* (also known as a living trust or inter vivos trust), the entire issue of probate is avoided. Instead, the property is transferred, or assets divided and disbursed, according to the terms of the trust. As the creator of the trust, you are the trustor, and you also name yourself as the original trustee, to manage your estate until your death. Upon your death, your *successor trustee* takes over. The successor trustee is responsible for making the disbursements. The successor trustee steps into the shoes of the original trustee to do the right thing, as if the trustee were alive and able to act for him- or herself.

Until the time of your passing, you are the manager of your estate and can make any changes or transfers. However, upon your death, the named successor takes over to carry out your wishes. Unlike your role during your lifetime, your successor can only follow the terms of the trust and must always act in the best interest of the trust. He or she cannot make any changes that would in any way detract from the intent of the trust.

In deciding whether a Will or Revocable Trust is appropriate for your estate planning needs, you are best advised to consult first with an attorney.

PRACTICAL POINT

There are many self-help books on the subject of Trusts available. However, my advice is to steer far away from Trust Seminars. Though an attorney may present the information, the seminars are often sponsored by an insurance company, which will try to sell insurance products that carry very high commissions and offer nothing to protect your estate. This matter is discussed more fully in Chapter 21.

Inheritance Taxes

Most people want to know if their estate will be taxed upon their death. The answer depends on the size of the estate. Federal taxes are owed only if your estate totaled more than $2 million in 2006 through 2008, or more than $3.5 million in 2009.

In 2010, the federal estate tax will disappear completely. However, in 2011, this exemption will revert back to $1 million unless Congress changes current law.

As a means of reducing federal tax liability, federal law permits you to give away as much as $12,000 a year, up to $1 million during your lifetime, to each of your children or to anyone else. This allows you to reduce your estate's tax liability. Prior to making any distributions, you should consult with an estate planning attorney.

State Laws

State inheritance tax laws vary. It is best to consult with an attorney to determine whether there will be any state tax liability owed by your estate.

CHAPTER 14:
LIVING WILLS

The document commonly known as a Living Will is probably the most misunderstood of all legal forms. It is often confused with a Last Will and Testament and an Advance Health Care Power of Attorney.

A Living Will is a document signed by you. Two persons must witness your signature, and some states also require that it be notarized. It is executed when you are of clear conscience, not under the influence of medication, and not acting under duress of another. It is your declaration that heroic measures should not be implemented to save your life.

Depending on what state you reside in, the document is also referred to as a Directive to a Physician or a Do Not Resuscitate order. All fifty states have laws authorizing doctors to follow your wishes as outlined in your Living Will. This means that adherence is mandatory rather than optional for doctors. Unlike an Advance Health Care Power of Attorney (discussed in Chapter 15), wherein you appoint someone to make health care decisions for you, the Living Will is almost always used to direct your doctor not to prolong your life.

When drafting estate planning documents for clients, attorneys routinely prepare a Living Will. However, when presented with this document, some clients hesitate to sign based on religious reasons. For example, the Roman Catholic Church views any attempt to terminate your life as suicide. Other client comments have included the following.

> ➤ I want to be given every opportunity to survive.
> ➤ I want to be kept alive long enough for a cure.
> ➤ Why should I make it easy for my doctors and nurses?

To set the record straight, a Living Will is not applicable if you have the sniffles. Your doctor will consider this document only if one of the following occurs:

> ➤ you are in a terminally ill condition *and* cannot breathe on your own, or
> ➤ after diagnostic testing, it is determined that there is no brain activity.

It is commonplace for hospitals, prior to admission, to inquire whether you have made such a document. Many hospitals have blank forms available. By having a Living Will on file with your doctor, you are shielding your family from having to make agonizing decisions.

Dan's Story

A few years back, a friend of mine suffered a brain aneurysm. Dan's father called me with the sad news and I went to the hospital to meet with the family. When I arrived, I was met by his wife, his parents, his sister, and brother. The tests showed no brain waves and while I was there, the attending doctor inquired with the family as to whether any decision had been made concerning suspending life support. Dan was hooked up to every tube imaginable, and his lifeless body was being kept alive by a respirator. After forty-eight agonizing hours, the family agreed to terminate life support. Dan had not prepared a Living Will, but I am sure he would not have wanted his family to endure the pain they went through in having to make that difficult decision.

Depending on your needs and comfort level, you can design a Living Will with language that requires specific events to occur before terminating artificial life support. For example, you can specify that certain testing be performed or that you be evaluated by specifically named doctors before a decision is made. Also, upon making such a decision, the Living Will can contain a provision directing that your organs be donated for transplantation. (see Chapter 3.)

Your Living Will can also specify your end-of-life decisions about whether or not you wish to have life-sustaining treatment, including:

➢ the use of antibiotics for infections;

➢ the use of artificial measures for providing nutrition and hydration (feeding tubes);

➢ the use of a ventilator or other mechanical means for assisting in breathing;

➢ blood transfusions;

➢ cardiopulmonary resuscitation in the event the heart stops beating; or,

➢ surgery.

Preparing a Living Will

A Living Will must be prepared correctly or it will not be enforceable. In addition, it is important that your treating doctor has a copy of the document. The following is a checklist for you follow in preparing your living will.

❍ Make sure that you sign and date your Living Will. Also, two individuals who are not related to you by marriage or blood must witness it. Some states also require that the document be notarized.

❍ Make copies of the Living Will and give a copy to your doctor to keep in your chart.

❍ Keep a copy of the document with your other estate planning documents. Make sure the person you have chosen to make health care decisions for you knows where your Living Will is being kept. Do not place it in a safe-deposit box.

❍ Review your Living Will every couple of years for any changes.

The following states have adopted their own standard Living Will forms.

Arizona	Kentucky	Ohio	West Virginia
Arkansas	Louisiana	Oregon	Wisconsin
California	Maine	Pennsylvania	Wyoming
Colorado	Minnesota	Rhode Island	
Connecticut	Mississippi	South Carolina	
Delaware	Missouri	Tennessee	
Florida	Montana	Texas	
Georgia	Nebraska	Utah	
Hawaii	Nevada	Vermont	
Idaho	New Hampshire	Virginia	
Illinois	New Jersey	Washington	

If you live in a state that has adopted a mandatory form, you can download that form by visiting **www.uslivingwillregistry.com**. Also, this website will electronically store your Living Will and make it available to your health care providers. Forms may also be available from your doctor, hospital, and long-term care facilities. You may also wish to consult with an attorney before completing this form. Another reference source that has forms available is **www.partnerhsipforcaring.org**. Their toll-free phone number is 800-658-8898.

If your state is not included in the list on page 105, you can use the form on pages 107–108.

PRACTICAL POINT

It is important that, after signing the document and having it notarized, a copy is provided to your treating physician for placement in your chart. Likewise, family members should be told that you have signed this document and should be advised as to where the original is being kept.

LIVING WILL (A DIRECTIVE TO MY PHYSICIAN)

I, _____, being of sound mind, willfully and voluntarily make known my desire that my dying not be artificially prolonged under the circumstances set forth below, and declare that:

If at any time I should have an incurable injury, disease, or illness certified to be a terminal condition by two physicians who have personally examined me, one of whom is my attending physician, and the physicians have determined that my death will occur unless life-sustaining procedures are used, and if the application of life-sustaining procedures would serve only to artificially prolong the dying process, I direct that life-sustaining procedures be withheld or withdrawn and that I be permitted to die naturally and with only the performance of medical procedures deemed necessary to provide me with comfort and care.

I further direct that if at any time I should be in a permanent vegetative state or an irreversible coma as certified by two physicians who have personally examined me, one of whom is my attending physician, and the physicians have determined that the application of life-sustaining procedures, including artificially administered food and fluid, will only artificially prolong my life in a permanent vegetative state or irreversible coma, I direct that these procedures, including the administration of food or fluids, be withheld or withdrawn, and that I be permitted to die naturally with only the administration of medication to alleviate pain or the performance of medical procedures necessary to provide me with comfort and care.

In the absence of my ability to give directions regarding the use of life-sustaining procedures, it is my intention that this Declaration be honored by my family and attending physician as the final expression of my legal right to refuse medical or surgical treatment and accept the consequences of such refusal.

I understand the full import of this Declaration, and I have emotional and mental capacity to make this declaration.

Dated: _____

_____ Signature

continued

State of _____

County of _____

On this _____ day of _____, 200____, before me, _____, a notary public in and for said county and state, residing herein, duly commissioned and sworn, personally appeared _____, personally known to me (or proved to me on the basis of satisfactory evidence) to be the person whose name is subscribed to the within instrument and acknowledged to me that he/she executed the same in his/her authorized capacity, and that by his/her signature on the instrument the person, or entity upon behalf of which the person acted, executed the instrument.

WITNESS my hand and official seal.

_____

Notary Public

CHAPTER 15:
POWERS OF ATTORNEY

The phrase *power of attorney* is defined as the appointment of someone to act on your behalf during your lifetime. It is a common misbelief that the power continues after one's death, when in fact, the power terminates upon one's passing.

David's Story

David gave a power of attorney to handle financial affairs to his son. The power included access to David's safe-deposit box. After David's death, his son appeared at the bank to retrieve the contents of the safe-deposit box. The vault teller denied him access, because she was aware that David had died. The son made a huge scene at the bank that almost resulted in his arrest. The bank, however, acted properly, as the power of attorney was no longer in effect.

The two most common powers of attorney are for advance health care and financial affairs. In some states, the Health Care Power of Attorney is referred to as a Health Care Directive and the Financial Power of Attorney is known as a Durable Power of Attorney.

Advance Health Care Power of Attorney

An *Advance Health Care Power of Attorney* may be general, allowing the appointee to make all health care decisions. Some states have broadened the powers of appointees to include issues regarding the end of life, such as withholding nourishment and making decisions for organ donation.

Terri's Story

The Florida Supreme Court made headlines a few years ago when it was required to determine the wishes of Terri Schiavo, a 40-year-old brain-damaged woman who had been tube-fed for almost fourteen years. Her husband requested that the hospital suspend providing nourishment for his wife, but she had not left a Living Will or Health Care Power of Attorney. The hospital initially complied with the request. However, the governor filed a brief with the court stating that the state had a "paramount interest in protecting the woman's health and safety, since she could not make decisions for herself." While the case was pending in the courts, nourishment was resumed. After months of arguing, the court decided that without a Living Will, not even her husband could decide what his wife's wishes were. Accordingly, the court ordered that the feeding tube remain indefinitely. Had Terri made clear, in writing, the medical treatment she did or did not want in the event she was unable to speak for herself, and had she designated a person she wished to make medical decisions for her, her name might be known only to her loved ones. After many appeals, including a petition to the United States Supreme Court to intervene, the Florida Court of Appeals reversed the lower court's position, allowing the feeding tube to be removed. Terry Schiavo passed away a few weeks after the court order was signed.

When a client consults with an attorney, it is part of the estate planning package to prepare both Health Care and Financial Powers of Attorney. Typically, the powers are not specific and are drafted in general terms. However, when a person is facing an immediate health crisis, and a physician has discussed risks or consequences of surgery, it is common to include specific language. For example, if you are facing exploratory surgery for a brain tumor, you might add instruction that in the event of you have to be placed on a ventilator due to a complication of the surgery, you do not want heroic measures to be taken to sustain your life artificially.

PRACTICAL POINT
Most Health Care Powers of Attorney are drafted so that the powers are only effective during the period of disability. Once the disability no longer exists, the powers terminate.

In almost all husband and wife situations, it is logical to choose your spouse to be the primary person to make health care decisions. However, most documents also require that a second person be named in the event the spouse is unavailable or also disabled.

Your appointee should be someone you trust and who knows your values. You should have previously discussed your advance health care planning goals with your appointee.

Your appointee should be a person who:
➢ will seek information and ask questions about your medical condition;
➢ will act as your health care advocate for your wishes even if it may mean challenging doctors who disagree;
➢ can make difficult decisions and think objectively when under stressful conditions;
➢ is available and willing to serve; and,
➢ will be sensitive to other loved ones' thoughts and will include them in discussions as needed.

Preparing Your Advance Health Care Power of Attorney

To be valid, an Advance Health Care Power of Attorney requires that all sections are fully completed. If a section is not completed, the validity of the document could be challenged. The following form may be adapted for your use. Closely follow the instructions provided.

DIRECTIONS FOR COMPLETING AN ADVANCE HEALTH CARE POWER OF ATTORNEY

Section

1.1   Type or print the name of your designated agent, and enter the county and state where the designated agent resides.

1.1(a)   Type or print the name of your designated alternate agent, and enter the county and state where the designated alternate agent resides.

2.1   Initial (a) or (b).

3.1   Initial (a) or (b) and strike out any choices in (c), or initial (d).

4.1   Type or print the name, address, and phone number of your physician.

5.2   Sign and date the form.

5.3   Have two witnesses print their names, include their addresses, and sign and date the form.

5.4   Have one witness complete this section (this witness must not be related to you).

5.5   Have your signature notarized.

EXPLANATION

You have the right to give instructions about your own health care. You also have the right to name someone else to make health care decisions for you. This form lets you do either or both of these things. It also lets you express your wishes regarding donation of organs and the designation of your primary physician.

Part 1 of this form is a power of attorney for health care. Part 1 lets you name another individual as agent to make health care decisions for you if you become incapable of making your own decisions, or if you want someone else to make those decisions for you now even though you are still capable. You may also name an alternate agent to act for you if your first choice is not willing, able, or reasonably available to make decisions for you. (Your agent may not be an operator or employee of a community care facility or a residential care facility where you are receiving care, or your supervising health care provider or employee of the health care institution where you are receiving care, unless your agent is related to you or is a coworker.)

Unless the form you sign limits the authority of your agent, your agent may make all health care decisions for you. This form has a place for you to limit the authority of your agent. You need not limit the authority of your agent if you wish to rely on your agent for all health care decisions that may have to be made. If you choose not to limit the authority of your agent, your agent will have the right to:

a. Consent or refuse consent to any care, treatment, service, or procedure to maintain, diagnose, or otherwise affect a physical or mental condition.

b. Select or discharge health care providers and institutions.

c. Approve or disapprove diagnostic tests, surgical procedures, and programs of medication.

d. Direct the provision, withholding, or withdrawal of artificial nutrition and hydration, and all other forms of health care, including cardiopulmonary resuscitation.

e. Make anatomical gifts, authorize an autopsy, and direct disposition of remains.

Part 2 of this form lets you give specific instructions about any aspect of your health care, whether or not you appoint an agent. Choices are provided for you to express your wishes regarding the provision, withholding, or withdrawal of treatment to keep you alive, as well as the provision of pain relief. Space is also provided for you to add to the choices you have made or for you to write out any additional wishes. If you are satisfied to allow your agent to determine what is best for you in making end-of-life decisions, you need not fill out Part 2 of this form.

Part 3 of this form lets you express an intention to donate your bodily organs and tissues following your death.

Part 4 of this form lets you designate a physician to have primary responsibility for your health care.

After completing this form, sign and date the form at the end.

The form must be signed by two qualified witnesses or acknowledged before a notary public. Give a copy of the signed and completed form to your physician, to any other health care providers you may have, to any health care institution at which you are receiving care, and to any health care agents you have named. You should talk to the person you have named as agent to make sure that he or she understands your wishes and is willing to take the responsibility.

You have the right to revoke this advance health care directive or replace this form at any time.

continued

POWER OF ATTORNEY FOR HEALTH CARE

PART 1

(1.1) **DESIGNATION OF AGENT:** I, _____, presently a resident of _____ County, state of _____, designate the following individual as my agent to make health care decisions for me: _____, presently a resident of _____ County, state of _____.

(1.1a) If I revoke my agent's authority or if my agent is not willing, able, or reasonably available to make a health care decision for me, I designate as my first alternate agent _____, presently a resident of _____ County, state of _____.

(1.2) **AGENT'S AUTHORITY:** My agent is authorized to make all health care decisions for me, including decisions to provide, withhold, or withdraw artificial nutrition and hydration and all other forms of health care to keep me alive, except as I state here:

_____

_____

_____

(Add additional sheets if needed.)

(1.3) **WHEN AGENT'S AUTHORITY BECOMES EFFECTIVE:** My agent's authority to make health care decisions for me takes effect immediately.

(1.4) **AGENT'S OBLIGATION:** My agent shall make health care decisions for me in accordance with this power of attorney for health care, any instructions I give in Part 2 of this form, and my other wishes to the extent known to my agent. To the extent my wishes are unknown, my agent shall make health care decisions for me in accordance with what my agent determines to be in my best interest. In determining my best interest, my agent shall consider my personal values to the extent known to my agent.

(1.5) **AGENT'S POST-DEATH AUTHORITY:** My agent is authorized to make anatomical gifts, authorize an autopsy, and direct disposition of my remains, except as I state here or in Part 3 of this form.

_____

_____

_____

(Add additional sheets if needed.)

(1.6) **NOMINATION OF CONSERVATOR:** If a conservator of my person needs to be appointed for me by a court, I nominate the agent designated in this form. If that agent is not willing, able, or reasonably available to act as conservator, I nominate the alternate agents whom I have named, in the order designated.

PART 2
INSTRUCTIONS FOR HEALTH CARE

If you fill out this part of the form, you may strike any wording you do not want.

(2.1) **END-OF-LIFE DECISIONS:** I direct that my health care providers and others involved in my care provide, withhold, or withdraw treatment in accordance with the choice I have initialed below:

_____(a) Choice Not To Prolong Life. I do not want my life to be prolonged if (1) I have an incurable and irreversible condition that will result in my death within a relatively short time, (2) I become unconscious and, to a reasonable degree of medical certainty, I will not regain consciousness, or (3) the likely risks and burdens of treatment would outweigh the expected benefits, OR

_____(b) Choice To Prolong Life. I want my life to be prolonged as long as possible within the limits of generally accepted health care standards.

(2.2) **RELIEF FROM PAIN:** Except as I state in the following space, I direct that treatment for alleviation of pain or discomfort be provided at all times, even if it hastens my death:

_____

_____

_____

(Add additional sheets if needed.)

(2.3) **OTHER WISHES:** (If you do not agree with any of the optional choices above and wish to write your own, or if you wish to add to the instructions you have given above, you may do so here.) I direct that:

_____

_____

_____

(Add additional sheets if needed.)

continued

PART 3
DONATION OF ORGANS AT DEATH
(OPTIONAL)

(3.1) Upon my death (initial applicable):

_____(a) I give any needed organs, tissues, or parts, OR

_____(b) I give the following organs, tissues, or parts:

_____

_____

_____ OR

_____(c) My gift is for the following purposes (strike out any of the following you do **not** want):

       (1) Transplant

       (2) Therapy

       (3) Research

       (4) Education

_____(d) I do not wish to donate my organs.

PART 4
PRIMARY PHYSICIAN
(OPTIONAL)

(4.1) I designate the following physician as my primary physician:

_____

(name of physician)

_____

(address)   (city)   (state)   (zip)

_____

(phone)

OPTIONAL: If the physician I have designated above is not willing, able, or reasonably available to act as my primary physician, I designate the following physician as my primary physician:

_____

(name of physician)

_____

(address)   (city)   (state)   (zip)

_____

(phone)

PART 5

(5.1) **EFFECT OF COPY**: A copy of this form has the same effect as the original.

(5.2) **SIGNATURE**: Sign and date the form here:

_____

Date _____

(5.3) **STATEMENT OF WITNESSES**: We declare under penalty of perjury under the laws of _____ (1) that the individual who signed or acknowledged this advance health care directive is personally known to me, or that the individual's identity was proven to me by convincing evidence, (2) that the individual signed or acknowledged this advance directive in my presence, (3) that the individual appears to be of sound mind and under no duress, fraud, or undue influence, (4) that I am not a person appointed as agent by this advance directive, and (5) that I am not the individual's health care provider, an employee of the individual's health care provider, the operator of a community care facility, an employee of an operator of a community care facility, the operator of a residential care facility for the elderly, or an employee of an operator of a residential care facility for the elderly.

Print Name: _____

Signature: _____

Address: _____

Dated: _____

Print Name: _____

Signature: _____

Address: _____

Dated: _____

continued

(5.4) ADDITIONAL STATEMENT OF WITNESSES: At least one of the above witnesses must also sign the following declaration. I further declare under penalty of perjury under the laws of the state of _____ that I am not related to the individual executing this advance health care directive by blood, marriage, or adoption, and to the best of my knowledge, I am not entitled to any part of the individual's Estate upon his or her death under a Will now existing or by operation of law.

_____

(signature of witness)

(5.5) STATE OF _____   )

COUNTY OF _____   )

On this _____ day of _____, 20_____ before me, a notary public in and for said county and state, residing herein, duly commissioned and sworn, personally appeared _____, personally known to me (or proved to me on the basis of satisfactory evidence) to be the person whose name is subscribed to the within instrument and acknowledged to me that he/she executed the same in his/her authorized capacity, and that by his/her signature on the instrument the person, or entity upon behalf of which the person acted, executed the instrument.

WITNESS my hand and official seal.

_____

(Signature of Notary Public)

Same-Sex Relationships

As mentioned in Chapter 3, your written designation of someone to make health care decisions for you if you are unable to make decisions for yourself will survive a court challenge by a family member. Specifically, if you are in a same-sex relationship, regardless of whether your family approves or disapproves, your choice for your partner to make decisions for you will be recognized by a court—providing the power of attorney was signed by you when you were competent to do so and not acting under the influence of someone else. The document must be properly prepared as recognized by your state law. This last requirement usually refers to whether the correct number of people witnessed your signing and whether it was required that your signature be notarized.

Marion's Story

Rachel had been living with her partner, Marion, for many years. On a rainy night, Marion lost control of her car driving home from work. The car skidded off the road and she was thrown from the vehicle. When she was brought to the hospital, she was in a coma and not responding to any stimulus. After receiving a call from the police, Rachel called Marion's parents. Immediately upon arriving at the hospital, the parents told Rachel that she had no place being there, as she was not immediate family. They said Marion was their daughter and they were in charge. The parents were Jehovah Witnesses and had already informed the attending physician that they were not authorizing any medical treatment—she was in God's hands. Rachel produced a copy of Marion's power of attorney, but Marion's parents laughed, saying their daughter must have been out of her mind to sign such a document. She would have only wanted her parents and God to be the final decision-makers of what was best for her health care. While Marion lay lifeless, breathing only with the help of a respirator, the physician told the family and Rachel that unless emergency surgery was performed to reduce the swelling of Rachel's brain, she would die. He felt that she had a reasonable chance of survival if the bleeding was stopped immediately. Rachel showed the power of attorney to the doctor over the objection of the parents. He then called the hospital administrator, who reviewed the document and said he was satisfied that Rachel had the lawful power to make health care decisions. Fortunately, there was a happy ending, as Marion survived the surgery and has since made a complete recovery.

Financial Power of Attorney

A Financial Power of Attorney, also known in some states as a Durable Power of Attorney, appoints someone to pay bills, endorse checks, and conduct other financial transactions. The power may be restricted to a specific transaction, such as selling a home, or it can authorize any kind of financial transaction. Depending upon how the power of attorney is written, the power can come into legal effect upon the occurrence of a disability, in which case it is sometimes referred to as a *Springing Power of Attorney*, because the power springs into action. Like the Health Care Power of Attorney, language can include that the power either continues or terminates once the disability no longer exists.

> PRACTICAL POINT
>
> Like the Advance Directive for Health Care, you may appoint an alternate person to have the financial power in the event the primary person is unavailable or disabled. The South Asian tsunami disaster of 2004 is an illustration of the importance of appointing an alternate name, as there were countless situations where both spouses were injured, and therefore, could not make health care or financial decisions for each other.

Preparing Your Financial Power of Attorney

Like the Health Care Power of Attorney, the Financial Power of Attorney requires that all sections are fully completed. If a section is not completed, the validity of the document could be challenged. The following form may be adapted for your use. Closely follow the instructions provided.

INSTRUCTIONS FOR COMPLETING THE DURABLE POWER OF ATTORNEY

Ⓐ Type or print your name in the first section, along with the country and state in which you live.

Ⓑ Type or print the name of the person that you nominate to be your Power of Attorney. Also include the county and state where that person resides.

Ⓒ Type or print (in section 22) the name of the alternate person that you nominate to be your Power of Attorney. Also include the county and state where that person resides.

Ⓓ Type or print (in section 23) your nominees for Conservator and Alternate Conservator.

Ⓔ Sign and date the document.

Ⓕ Have your signature notarized.

DURABLE POWER OF ATTORNEY

WARNING TO PERSON EXECUTING THIS DOCUMENT:

THIS IS AN IMPORTANT LEGAL DOCUMENT. IT CREATES A DURABLE POWER OF ATTORNEY THAT BECOMES EFFECTIVE ON YOUR INCAPACITY AS HEREAFTER SET FORTH. BEFORE EXECUTING THIS DOCUMENT, YOU SHOULD KNOW THESE IMPORTANT FACTS.

1. THIS DOCUMENT MAY PROVIDE THE PERSON YOU DESIGNATE AS YOUR ATTORNEY-IN-FACT WITH BROAD POWERS TO DISPOSE, SELL, CONVEY, AND ENCUMBER YOUR REAL AND PERSONAL PROPERTY.

2. THESE POWERS WILL EXIST FOR AN INDEFINITE PERIOD OF TIME UNLESS YOU LIMIT THEIR DURATION IN THIS DOCUMENT. THESE POWERS WILL CONTINUE TO EXIST NOTWITHSTANDING YOUR SUBSEQUENT DISABILITY OR INCAPACITY.

3. YOU HAVE THE RIGHT TO REVOKE OR TERMINATE THIS DURABLE POWER OF ATTORNEY AT ANY TIME.

POWER OF ATTORNEY TO BECOME EFFECTIVE
ONLY ON INCAPACITY OF PRINCIPAL

This durable power of attorney shall become effective only on the incapacity of the undersigned principal. The undersigned shall conclusively be deemed incapacitated for purposes of this instrument when the agent receives a written and signed opinion from a licensed physician that the principal is physically or mentally incapable of managing the principal's finances. Such written opinion, when received, shall be attached to this instrument. Third parties may rely on the agent's authority without further evidence of incapacity when this instrument is presented with such physician's statement attached. No licensed physician who executes a medical opinion of incapacity shall be subject to liability because of such execution. The principal hereby waives any privilege that may apply to release of information included in such medical opinion.

While the principal is not incapacitated, this durable power of attorney may be modified by the principal at any time by written notice given by the principal to the agent and may be terminated at any time by either the principal or the agent by written notice given by the terminating party to the other party.

This power of attorney shall continue after the principal's incapacity in accordance with its terms.

On the death of the principal, this power shall terminate and the assets of the principal shall be distributed to the duly appointed personal representative of the principal's estate; or, if no estate is being administered, to the persons who lawfully take the assets without the necessity of administration when they have supplied the agent with satisfactory documents as provided by law.

TO WHOM IT MAY CONCERN:

Ⓐ _____, the principal, presently a resident of _____ County, state of _____, hereby appoints Ⓑ _____, presently a resident of _____ County, state of _____, as the principal's true and lawful attorney-in-fact for the principal and in the principal's name, place, and stead on the principal's incapacity:

1. To manage, control, lease, sublease, and otherwise act concerning any real property that the principal may own, collect and receive rents or income therefrom, pay taxes, charges, and assessments on the same, repair, maintain, protect, preserve, alter, and improve the same and do all things necessary or expedient to be done in the agent's judgment in connection with the property.

2. To manage and control all partnership interests owned by the principal and to make all decisions the principal could make as a general partner, limited partner, or both, and to execute all documents required of the principal as such partner, all to the extent that the agent's designation for such purposes is allowed by law and is not in contravention of any partnership or other agreement.

3. To purchase, sell, invest, reinvest, and generally deal with all stocks, bonds, debentures, warrants, partnership interests, rights, and securities owned by the principal.

4. To collect and deposit for the benefit of the principal all debts, interest, dividends, or other assets that may be due or belong to the principal and to execute and deliver receipts and other discharges therefore; to demand, arbitrate, and pursue litigation on the principal's behalf concerning all rights and benefits to which the principal may be entitled; and to compromise, settle, and discharge all such matters as the agent considers appropriate under the circumstances.

5. To pay any sums of money that may at any time is or become owing from the principal, to sell, and to adjust and compromise any claims which may be made against the principal as the agent considers appropriate under the circumstances.

6. To grant, sell, transfer, mortgage, deed in trust, pledge and otherwise deal in all property, real and personal, that the principal may own, including but not limited to any real property described on any exhibit attached to this instrument including property acquired after execution of this instrument; to attach exhibits to this instrument that provide legal descriptions of all such property; and to execute such instruments as the agent deems proper in conjunction with all matters covered in this paragraph 6.

7. To prepare and file all income and other federal and state tax returns that the principal is required to file; to sign the principal's name; hire preparers and advisors and pay for their services; and to do whatever is necessary to protect the principal's assets from assessments for income taxes and other taxes to receive confidential information; to receive checks in payment of any refund of taxes, penalties, or interest; to execute waivers (including offers of waivers) of restrictions on assessment or collection of tax deficiencies and waivers of notice of disallowance of claims for credit or refund; to execute consents extending the statutory period for assessment or collection of taxes; to execute closing agreements under Internal Revenue Code section 7121 or any successor statute; and to delegate authority or substitute another representative with respect to all above matters.

8. To deposit in and draw on any checking, savings, agency, or other accounts that the principal may have in any banks, savings and loan associations, and any accounts with securities brokers or other commercial institutions, and to establish and terminate all such accounts.

continued

9. To invest and reinvest the principal's funds in every kind of property, real, personal, or mixed, and every kind of investment, specifically including, but not limited to, corporate obligations of every kind, preferred or common stocks, shares of investment trusts, investment companies, and mutual funds, and mortgage participations that, under the circumstances then prevailing (specifically including but not limited to the general economic conditions and the principal's anticipated needs), persons of skill, prudence, and diligence acting in a similar capacity and familiar with those matters would use in the conduct of an enterprise of a similar character and with similar aims, to attain the principal's goals; and to consider individual investments as part of an overall plan.

10. To have access to all safe-deposit boxes in the principal's name or to which the principal is an authorized signatory; to contract with financial institutions for the maintenance and continuation of safe-deposit boxes in the principal's name; to add to and remove the contents of all such safe-deposit boxes; and to terminate contracts for all such safe-deposit boxes.

11. To make additions and transfer assets to any and all living revocable trusts of which the principal is a settlor.

12. To make direct payments to the provider for tuition and medical care for the principal's issue under Internal Revenue Code section 3503(e) or any successor statute, which excludes such payments from gift tax liability.

13. To use any credit cards in the principal's name to make purchases and to sign charge slips on behalf of the principal as may be required to use such credit cards; and to close the principal's charge accounts and terminate the principal's credit cards under circumstances where the agent considers such acts to be in the principal's best interest.

14. Generally to do, execute, and perform any other act, deed, matter, or thing, that in the opinion of the agent ought to be done, executed, or performed in conjunction with this power of attorney, of every kind and nature, as fully and effectively as the principal could do if personally present. The enumeration of specific items, acts, rights, or powers does not limit or restrict, and is not to be construed or interpreted as limiting or restricting, the general powers granted to the agent except where powers are expressly restricted.

15. The agent is authorized and directed to commence enforcement proceedings, at the principal's expense, against any third party who fails to honor this durable power of attorney.

16. Notwithstanding any other possible language to the contrary in this document, the agent is specifically NOT granted the following powers:

(a) To use the principal's assets for the agent's own legal obligations, including but not limited to support of the agent's dependents;

(b) To exercise any trustee powers under an irrevocable trust of which the agent is a settlor and the principal is a trustee; and,

(c) To exercise incidents of ownership over any life insurance policies that the principal owns on the agent's life.

17. Any third party from whom the agent may request information, records, or other documents regarding the principal's personal affairs may release and deliver all such information, records, or documents to the agent. The principal hereby waives any privilege that may apply to release of such information, records, or other documents.

18. The agent's signature under the authority granted in this power of attorney may be accepted by any third party or organization with the same force and effect as if the principal were personally present and acting on the principal's own behalf. No person or organization who relies on the agent's authority under this instrument shall incur any liability to the principal, the principal's estate, heirs, successors, or assigns, because of reliance on this instrument.

19. The principal's estate, heirs, successors, and assigns shall be bound by the agent's acts under this power of attorney.

20. This power of attorney shall commence and take effect on the principal's subsequent disability or incapacity as set forth above.

21. The principal hereby ratifies and confirms all that the agent shall do, or cause to be done, by virtue of this power of attorney.

22. If the named attorney-in-fact is for any reason unwilling or unable so to serve, then the principal hereby nominates © _____, presently a resident of _____ County, state of _____, as the principal's true and lawful attorney-in-fact.

23. If a conservatorship of the principal's person or estate or both is deemed necessary, the principal hereby nominates Ⓓ _____ as conservator of the principal's person and estate. If _____ is for any reason unwilling or unable so to serve, the principal hereby nominates _____ as such conservator.

On the appointment of a conservator of the principal's estate, this power of attorney shall terminate and the agent shall deliver the assets of the principal under the agent's control as directed by the conservator of the principal's estate.

Ⓔ IN WITNESS WHEREOF, the principal has signed this springing durable power of attorney on _____.

_____
(Signature)

Ⓕ STATE OF _____
COUNTY OF _____

On this _____ day of _____, 200____, before me, _____, a notary public in and for said county and state, residing herein, duly commissioned and sworn, personally appeared _____ personally known to me (or proved to me on the basis of satisfactory evidence) to be the person whose name is subscribed to the within instrument and acknowledged to me that he/she executed the same in his/her authorized capacity, and that by his/her signature on the instrument the person, or entity upon behalf of which the person acted, executed the instrument.

WITNESS my hand and official seal.

_____
(Signature of Notary Public)

Conservatorships

A Conservator is someone who is appointed by the court to manage your affairs. A Conservator may be appointed if you become unable to make sound decisions, feed or dress yourself, handle your finances, or resist people who attempt to unduly influence you.

Conservators may be family members or friends. In some cases, the court may be required to appoint a Conservator, known as the Public Guardian. Unlike the person you appoint as your Power of Attorney, the court oversees and supervises the Conservator's handling of your financial affairs. Further, the Conservator may require compensation, especially if the court makes the appointment, and the fees (for which your estate is responsible) can be expensive.

Conservatorship appointments typically occur when a family member fears that someone (the proposed Conservatee) is not taking care of him- or herself or is making imprudent decisions. Upon the filing of a petition, the court will inquire as to the Conservatee's competency and decide whether the petition should be granted.

You can designate your own Conservator in your Advance Health Care Power of Attorney, to be used by a court for future consideration. Further, even if a conservatorship action is filed, you can nominate a Conservator if you do not consent to the appointment of the person who has filed the petition. Of course, the court needs to determine that you are competent to make such a nomination.

CHAPTER 16:
NAVIGATING THROUGH THE PAPERWORK

Part of planning for the inevitable includes organizing your financial records. For most, this is easier said than done, as many of us stuff cancelled checks, investment statements, and other important papers into cabinets and drawers without giving a second thought about what we would do if we should need immediate access to that information.

Organizing Your Financial Records

In organizing your files, it is best to designate folders by category. The following are some of the main categories you will need.

> *Insurance*—life, health, disability, long-term health, automobile, home, and other policies
> *Investment*—brokerage statements, certificates of deposit, savings bonds, and other long-term investments
> *Retirement*—IRAs, 401(k)s, annuities, pensions, Social Security earnings statements, and other retirement information
> *Personal Data*—Social Security cards, passports, any alien registration documentation, birth certificates, adoption records, and other court records
> *Income*—tax returns and supporting documentation
> *Certificates of Title*—vehicle registration and title, home and other real estate deeds

This information can also be stored electronically on your computer. However, it is best to have the information also stored on a floppy disk or CD, and stored in a safe place.

When organizing your files, complete the following form, which details where your important records are located.

PERSONAL DATA AND RECORD LOCATOR

PERSONAL DATA

Social Security Number _____ - _____ - _____

Phone Number _____

Email Address _____@_____

Fax Number _____

Driver's License Number _____

PROPOSED GUARDIAN OF MINOR CHILD/CHILDREN

Name _____

Address _____

Phone Number _____

Relationship to Child/Children _____

LEGAL AND FINANCIAL ADVISORS

Name of Attorney _____

Phone Number _____

Name of Accountant _____

Phone Number _____

Name of Trustee/Executor _____

Phone Number _____

Name of Insurance Agent _____

Phone Number _____

Name of Financial Advisor/Stockbroker _____

Phone Number _____

LOCATION OF DOCUMENTS

Personal Address Book _____

Estate Planning Documents (Will, Trust, Living Will, Powers of Attorney, Legacy Will) _____

Organ Donor Cards _____

Deeds/Titles to Real Estate and Personal Property _____

Income Tax Records _____

Vital Statistics (Birth Certificate, Marriage License, Military Records) _____

_____

Funeral/Cemetery Contracts _____

Medical Records _____

Insurance Policies _____

Investment Certificates (Stocks, Bonds, 401(k), IRA, Pension, etc.) _____

_____

Vehicle (Auto/RV/Boat) Registration _____

Bank Statements _____

Credit Card Records _____

Insurance Policies _____

Extra Keys _____

Pet Records _____

continued

Contracts _____
Home Repairs/Warranties _____
Vehicle Maintenance _____
Frequent Flyer Miles _____
Passports/Social Security Cards _____
Unfinished Business (Leases, Contracts, Moneys Owed to You) _____
_____
Location of Home Safe _____
Ongoing Divorce or Other Court Proceedings/Judgments _____
_____
Trademarks, Copyrights, Patents, and Other Important Papers _____
_____
Safe-Deposit Records _____
Location of Key to Safe-Deposit Box _____
_____ at _____ Bank

PERSONAL COMPUTER ACCESSIBILITY
Screen Name _____
Password _____

EMPLOYMENT
Name of Employer _____
Phone Number _____
Immediate Supervisor _____
Benefits Dept. Phone Number _____

PERSONS TO NOTIFY UPON DEATH
Name _____ Phone Number _____
Name _____ Phone Number _____
Name _____ Phone Number _____
Name _____ Phone Number _____

ORGANIZATIONS TO BE NOTIFIED UPON DEATH
Name _____
Phone Number _____
Contact Person _____

Name _____
Phone Number _____
Contact Person _____

Name _____
Phone Number _____
Contact Person _____

PRACTICAL POINT
The IRS has three years to challenge a tax return from the date it was filed and six years to audit any return for allegedly unreported income. As a result, accountants and tax preparers recommend that tax returns and supporting documentation be kept for at least seven years.

Organizing Your Credit Accounts

Access to your credit card and other account information may be invaluable to your survivors, as it will allow those persons that you have placed in a position of trust to immediately make changes so the estate can avoid incurring further expenses. For example, if you subscribe to an Internet provider such as AOL, you may have prearranged to have your credit card billed monthly for the service. If your representative knows your password and user name, he or she can immediately cancel the service.

It is a tremendous task trying to remember passwords and other identifying information that allows us to access our personal information via the Internet or by phone. If you have ever called your bank's automated phone center, the prompt asks for your personal identification number, and if you forgot it, forget it. Even when a live operator comes on the line, the questioning you are put through can be brutal.

Nate's Story

Nate's son Victor lived out of state. Victor had been out of work for six months and his financial situation was bleak. He was able to borrow money for the plane ticket. Upon arriving in California, Victor contacted me. Nate had told him that he had made a Will and there was a savings account with $30,000. Victor went through Nate's papers and found the ATM card for the account and a bank statement that provided the account number. However, Nate had not left the PIN for the card. Upon arriving at the bank, the account manager asked to see a death certificate, which Victor did not have, as he was told that such certificates are not issued until ten days after death. The bank was correct in withholding access to the funds. However, had Nate provided the PIN number

continued

for the ATM card, Victor would have had access to funds to pay for the funeral and other related expenses. Instead, Nate's body remained at the county morgue for several weeks.

The best solution is to make a list of all credit card accounts by name, account number, customer service number, and (if you have set these up) passwords and user names or PIN numbers. In addition, if you have merchants that automatically bill your credit card monthly, add them to a separate list by name, account number, and customer service number, along with any passwords and user names. The most common types of merchants that you may have arrangements for automatic billing are:

> Internet providers;
> fitness clubs;
> insurance policies;
> newspapers; and,
> charities.

Also, take inventory of any reoccurring utilities that you have arranged for automatic billing, such as for phone, gas, and electric service. These providers should also be listed.

The challenge, however, is how to make this information available to your survivors and still safeguard it so as to avoid it from getting into the wrong hands. To keep it safe, once you have organized this information, place it in a sealed envelope along with your other important documents, and tell your representative where it is being kept. For your convenience, an Accounts Organizer follows.

PRACTICAL POINT

If you have a safe-deposit box, you may want to store all of this information in the box, provided your representative can also sign on the box to gain access. Otherwise, upon your passing, the box will be sealed and your representative will only be able to obtain its contents with a court order.

ACCOUNTS ORGANIZER

List All Non-Tax-Deferred Accounts (Savings, Checking, Credit Union, Brokerage, CDs, Treasury Bills, Other)

Name	Value	Account #

List All Tax-Deferred Accounts (IRA, 401(k), Pension, Profit, Sharing, Keoghs, Tax-Deferred Annuities, Other)

Name	Value	Account #

List All Insurance Benefits (Military, Life, Home, Disability, Long-Term Care, Medical, Auto, Other)

Company	Policy #	Beneficiary

FREQUENT FLYER MILES

Many frequent flyer programs allow you to transfer miles in to your spouse and other family members. The airlines will require a copy of a death certificate and written documentation from you assigning the miles in your account. You can make written provision for the transfer in your Will or Trust.

Name of Airline Program	Account #	Customer Service #

continued

List All Obligations (Home, Vacation Home, Time-Share, Automobile, Boat, Motorcycle, RV Loans, Bank Credit Cards, Department Stores, Other)

Name	Account #	Customer Service #

List All Checking Account Automatic Deductions (Internet, Cable, Satellite, Cell Phone, Newspapers, Insurance, Fitness Club, and Other Memberships)

Name	Account #	Customer Service #

CHAPTER 17:
MANAGING DEBT

If you are living on a fixed or more limited income due to unexpected costs of medical treatment and prescription drugs, it is not uncommon for your other debts to become unmanageable. How you handle this situation depends on your particular circumstance.

If you are having trouble paying your bills, contact your creditors and ask for more time to make payments. If you want professional help in reorganizing your debts, the nonprofit National Foundation of Consumer Credit (800-388-2227, **www.nfcc.org**) will provide counseling and guidance in helping you work out plans for repayment to your creditors.

Be leery of the many companies that advertise debt consolidation services. Their fees are very high, and they often apply any money you pay to their fees before paying any of your creditors. Also, be very cautious about obtaining a debt consolidation loan to pay off your creditors. If the interest rate is too high, you could wind up owing a lot more than the original amount of your debts. If you do get a loan, make sure that the financial statements you provide to the lender are true and correct.

Who Gets Paid

There are two types of debts—secured and unsecured. Unsecured debts are the common MasterCards, Visas, and Discover Cards, as well as most department stores. They are unsecured because although you may have made purchases or obtained services, the creditors to whom you owe the money do not hold anything of yours as collateral. As such, they would need to first get a judgment against you before they could proceed to enforce the debt.

Secured debts are those in which you have either pledged specific property as collateral or financed the purchase using specific property as collateral. The two most common examples of secured debts are home mortgages and car purchases. In both cases, the property is the collateral, so the creditor can place a lien on the home or repossess the vehicle to enforce the debt.

One question everyone has is, "who would be responsible for my debts if I do not pay them and pass away?" The answer depends on whether there are assets to satisfy payment to your creditors. For example, if you have $30,000 in credit card debts and have a home with equity, the creditors can file claims against your estate for payment from the proceeds of the sale of any assets. If, however, there is no estate to be probated, the creditors will have no recourse for payment and, therefore, will not get paid.

PRACTICAL POINT

Credit insurance is a type of insurance that pays your debts if you should become disabled and unable to work. Some policies cover your home mortgage, while others are applicable to consumer debts such as automobiles and credit cards. Many credit card companies offer these policies as an add-on fee to your monthly credit card bill. Before committing to such a policy, compare premiums with other companies, as the costs of such policies can be very expensive.

Is Filing for Bankruptcy an Option?

If you have few assets and little or no income, you may consider filing for bankruptcy. There are two types of personal bankruptcy—Chapter 13 and Chapter 7. In general, if you have a steady income, Chapter 13 allows you to stop all debt collection in exchange for your promise to pay your available income (after payment of expenses) as part of a three- to five-year repayment plan. Under Chapter 7, however, you are asking the bankruptcy court to cancel most of your debts because you do not have enough money or property to pay them off. If you have secured debts, like a car or home, you still will need to continue the payment obligation on the debt that is secured by the property. Otherwise, the creditor can exercise its rights to obtain its collateral.

State laws vary greatly as to what property you may keep and still claim bankruptcy, so you should consult with a bankruptcy attorney before making any decision about filing.

Tom's Story

Tom was diagnosed with inoperable lung cancer. In addition, he was severely overweight and suffered from high blood pressure. He was overextended with credit card debts while he was working. With his recent diagnosis, he was advised to quit his employment so that he could address his medical issues. Upon consulting with our office, he was advised that if he filed bankruptcy, he could eliminate more than $65,000 he had in credit card debt. Tom followed our advice. Soon thereafter, he began a program of both chemotherapy and radiation, which, according to his doctors, extended his life by at least two years—long enough to see his daughter's high school graduation. He credited the bankruptcy filing with relieving the stress associated with his bill obligations. I cite this example not to condone bankruptcy filings in total disregard of your debts, but instead to illustrate how removing the pressures associated with owing bills may allow you to better concentrate on end-of-life decisions.

CHAPTER 18:
PRIVATE INSURANCE AND FINANCIAL PLANNING

In planning for the inevitable, part of the process should include developing an income stream should you reach a point where you are unable to work. This would allow you to pay your normal monthly expenses and any increased expenses related to your care. Reverse mortgages allow you to borrow against the equity in your home. In addition, there are several types of insurance that provide income if you are unable to work.

Reverse Mortgages

We save for our retirement. However, despite the best insurance available, most people faced with a terminal illness are often not prepared to financially handle the costs of medicine and other expenses associated with the illness. Reverse mortgages may be a viable solution to provide additional income, as you may borrow against the equity in your home. Further, the loan does not have to be repaid until after one's passing.

Reverse mortgages were first introduced in the early 1990s. Before then, a person who owned equity would have had to sell his or her home or borrow against the real estate if he or she needed money. Borrowing against the home was not always the best solution, as the loan required that payments commence immediately. Of course, if you were ill and not working, it would be difficult—if not impossible—to make a loan payment. As a result, many people in this position had to sell their homes and relocate.

Unlike a traditional home loan, which requires monthly payments, a reverse mortgage does not have to be paid back for as long as you reside in your home. Further, the amount that you can borrow may be borrowed in one lump sum payment, or you can elect to receive advances at monthly or other intervals. The loan is repaid with interest when you either sell your home, permanently move from your residence, or pass away. If you are married, most reverse mortgages include language that says the loan does not have to be repaid until the last living borrower dies. However, you must keep in mind that a reverse mortgage is a loan against your home and eventually does have to be repaid.

PRACTICAL POINT
Reverse mortgages may have tax consequences to both you (the borrower) and your estate. It is best to consult with your estate financial planner or an attorney before applying for the loan.

Even though you are not making monthly payments, the amount that you or your estate will eventually owe grows larger each month, as more is borrowed and interest is added to the balance of the loan. Likewise, if you decide to sell your home, the amount of your net proceeds (the amount you would receive after all loans against your home are paid) is reduced each time you borrow money against your home. However, by law, the amount owed on the reverse mortgage can never be larger than the value of your home.

PRACTICAL POINT
Title to the real estate remains in your name. Therefore, as the owner, you are still required to pay all real property taxes and maintain insurance. Further, if you should default on either of these obligations, the lender of the reverse mortgage has the legal ability to call the loan due and foreclose against the property.

Supplemental Security Income

If you are receiving benefits from *Supplemental Security Income* (SSI), Medicare, or other public benefits, the proceeds from a reverse mortgage could affect your eligibility to continue to receive benefits, since the money that you will receive is viewed as an asset. For example, SSI allows you to have only $2,000 in assets, excluding real estate.

You can obtain more information on reverse mortgages by visiting the U.S. Department of Housing and Urban Development's website at **www.hud.gov.**

Disability Insurance

Similar to a reverse mortgage, disability insurance will provide income should you become ill and unable to perform your usual occupation. It is a replacement for your lost income from being unable to work. Depending on the policy, disability insurance typically replaces 50% of what was your gross income (your wages before taxes are withheld). The benefits that are paid from the disability policy are tax-free (the benefits do not have to be reported as income on your tax returns).

Before a policy is issued, the applicant must be in generally good health. Further, depending on your age at the time the policy is applied for, the insurance company may also require a physical examination at its expense, as well as your authorization for it to contact your doctor to review your medical records.

Defining Disability

The definition of total disability differs from policy to policy. The most liberal definition of total disability is called *own-occupation disability*. To meet this definition, all that is required is that you show medical proof that you cannot perform your present job, regardless of whether you can do some other type of work. The strictest definition of total disability is known as *any-occupation disability*. To receive benefits, you must prove that you are medically unable to perform any type of work. If you have any questions concerning the language in the policy, have it reviewed by an attorney.

Long-Term Care Insurance

With the average daily cost of home health care being $140, many people have elected to purchase long-term care insurance. This type of policy will pay home, assisted living, and nursing care expenses. Basically, depending upon the type of policy you purchase, the insurance company agrees to pay up to a certain daily amount for your care.

This is not health insurance. It does not pay health care providers, such as doctors and hospitals. Instead, it covers the costs of people who are assisting with your daily needs, like bathing and feeding.

People mainly purchase this type of policy because they have savings and investments that they do not want to touch. Others purchase it so that they do not burden their children with having to pay such expenses.

John and Shelly's Story

For the majority of their lives, John and Shelly enjoyed good health and maintained an active lifestyle. However, in their 90s, daily chores were becoming more and more difficult for them. Shelly was having problems seeing, which made driving a challenge. John was suffering from arthritis, which was interfering with his walking. Steadily, their abilities to care for themselves and each other deteriorated. All of their family lived out of state, and it was suggested that they consider moving to an assisted living facility, but they opposed this option, saying they wanted to remain in their home. Instead, for over two years, 24-hour care was maintained in their home to the tune of over $450,000. They were able to afford the expense, but it greatly reduced the value of their estate. Had a long-term care policy been taken out many years ago when they were both medically eligible, it would have covered their assisted living expenses.

Before a policy is issued, the insurance company will review your medical history. You must be in reasonably good health. If you do have a preexisting condition that in all probability will require long-term care, such as Alzheimer's disease, no company will issue you a policy, because there is a greater probability that the insurance company will pay out more in benefits than it would receive in premiums.

In determining whether purchasing long-term care insurance is right for you, consider the cost of the premiums and your ability to pay those premiums for the rest of your life or until you medically qualify to receive benefits. Because of the costs, these policies have the highest rate of cancellation.

Most long-term care insurance carriers do not pay benefits for:
➤ mental diseases and nervous disorders, other than Alzheimer's;
➤ addictions to drugs and alcohol;
➤ injuries and illnesses caused by war;
➤ treatment paid by the government; or,
➤ injuries that are self-inflicted, such as suicide attempts.

> ### PRACTICAL POINT
> Disability insurance protects your income. Long-term care insurance pays for the cost of your care. Though they are similar in design, disability pays on your ability to work and long-term care pays on your ability to do daily activities (such as eat, dress, and bathe). If you can afford both, get both.

Funeral Insurance

Although funeral insurance does not provide income, it does protect you and your family against the inevitable costs when a family member passes away. If you have insurance for a funeral, you have the peace of mind that you provided for the unexpected costs of a funeral or cremation.

When shopping for a policy, the following questions should be asked.
➤ What is covered by the policy?
➤ What is the cost for coverage?
➤ What is not covered?
➤ Are there additional riders that can be added to the policy to cover all expenses?
➤ How much will the premiums be for an individual policy as opposed to a family policy?
➤ How long has the company been issuing such policies? Does it pay out claims efficiently, and what is its service record like?
➤ Is there a waiting period?
➤ Does the policy have an expiration date?

Further, look for a policy that has a cost of living acceleration clause that will cover increased costs in the future.

Life Insurance

Unless you have the type of life insurance that allows you to borrow against the policy's value (known as whole life insurance), life insurance does not provide income during your lifetime. If you were to become ill, insurance companies would generally not consider you for issuing a policy.

However, members of the American Association of Retired Persons (AARP) can apply for a guaranteed life insurance policy regardless of their health. Benefits are paid up to $15,000, and the insurance company does not require a health examination. For more information, visit **www.aarp.org**.

PRACTICAL POINT

If you have been diagnosed with a terminal illness and your life expectancy is less than six months, there are insurance companies that will pay you the face value of your insurance policy, less a substantial discount. This is known as a *viatical settlement*. In a sense, the company buys your policy from you at a discount, and then receives the face amount of your policy upon your death from the company that originally issued you the policy. An Internet search of the key words "viatical settlements" will produce many sites.

Travel Insurance

If your business requires you to do extensive air travel, or you are fortunate enough to spend a lot of leisure time away from home, travel insurance specifically insures against travel-related accidents and death. Airport terminals often have kiosks with applications. If you have taken a cruise or purchased a vacation package, travel agents will offer travel insurance as an add-on to the cost of your vacation. Though such policies do not provide income, in the event of sudden death, benefits are payable to your beneficiaries.

CHAPTER 19:
MEDICARE AND SOCIAL SECURITY DISABILITY

Chapter 18 discusses private insurance options that may be available to help defray the cost of health care and provide for income to cover your expenses if you cannot work. However, there are two federal insurance programs that are also available.

Medicare

Medicare is a federal health insurance program that primarily covers Social Security recipients who are at least 65 years of age, individuals under 65 who have long-term disabilities, and those who need kidney dialysis or a kidney transplant. Your income level and assets have no bearing on your eligibility for coverage.

The program has two main components. Part A is referred to as hospital insurance. It covers inpatient hospital care, some skilled nursing and home health care, and hospice care. Part B helps pay for additional therapy and some medically necessary home health care.

Generally, Medicare participants can choose between managed care plans, known as Medicare HMOs, and fee-for-service coverage, such as Blue Cross plans. Regardless of the plan chosen, the participant pays deductibles, co-payments, and in some cases, a monthly premium. Medicare then pays the remainder. In addition, Medicare recipients also must pay a monthly premium that is deducted directly from their monthly Social Security check.

Social Security Disability Benefits

If you are unable to work due to a medical illness, you may be entitled to receive Social Security Disability benefits. You do not have to be age 65 or older to qualify. As long as you had Social Security benefits withheld from your wages, you may qualify.

What is Social Security Disability?

Social Security Disability is a federal program that provides benefits to people who are unable to work. In order to receive benefits, you must prove that you have a physical or mental impairment that prevents you from doing any substantial gainful work, and the disability must be expected to last or has lasted at least twelve months, or is expected to result in death.

This definition of disability has been developed by the Social Security Administration, and is used as a guideline in determining whether a claimant is found to be disabled. Because the definition is subject to interpretation, proving that one is disabled is often difficult. This is why so many claimants are initially denied, only to have their claim approved when it is heard by a judge.

Claim Procedures

If you meet the definition of disability, file an initial application at any local Social Security district office. An application may also be made over the phone by calling 800-772-1213, or you can visit **www.ssa.gov** and file online. The person applying for benefits is known as the *claimant*. If you are physically or mentally unable to file on your own, you can appoint someone to file the paperwork and act on your behalf. That person is known as your *representative payee*.

Along with the application, the claimant is also required to provide medical records that support the claimant's belief that he or she is disabled. These records must be filed along with your application. Social Security will contact your treating doctors for additional information. After the file is opened at the local Social Security district office, the file is sent to the state department of disability services to determine your eligibility to receive benefits. Depending on the nature of the disability, you may be required to see a Social Security doctor at no expense to you.

If the case is approved, you will receive a letter notifying you of the amount of your monthly benefits. In addition, you are entitled to receive medical insurance benefits, such as Medicare.

Request for Reconsideration (The First Appeal)

Most claimants are denied benefits upon their initial application. Statistics show that more than 70% of initial claims are denied. There are several reasons for this very high percentage, including:

> ➤ the claimant worked (was gainfully employed) in the last twelve months;
> ➤ the claimant provided no medical proof of his or her disability;
> ➤ the claimant failed to appear at a scheduled medical examination; or,
> ➤ the claimant's disability is materially as a result of alcohol or drug abuse (under new Social Security Disability regulations, alcohol and drug dependency is no longer a disability).

For most claimants, however, they are denied because the definition of disability is subject to interpretation. In addition, too often a decision is made based on the claimant's written responses to the questions asked on the initial application for Social Security benefits. This application alone does not always reveal the true picture of the claimant's disability. As a result, people who are clearly disabled are denied.

The following are excerpts taken from actual Social Security denial letters.

Though you complain about tightness in your chest, difficulty with breathing, and are on a waiting list for a heart transplant, it does not appear that your condition will last for twelve months, and therefore, you are not disabled.

Though you have a compression fracture of your back, had surgery during which rods and plates were inserted, are depressed, and have pain...you can still do sedentary work.

Though you have been diagnosed with leukemia and are receiving chemotherapy, your condition does not appear disabling.

Though you have mental problems, have attempted suicide multiple times, and are receiving psychiatric care, you are able to follow simple directions and can perform your past work as a child care provider.

A claimant who disagrees with the initial decision must appeal the decision by filing a form entitled *Request for Reconsideration* within sixty days of receiving the denial letter. Upon receipt of the Request for Reconsideration, the file is again reviewed by the district office to determine if the first decision was incorrect. Often, at this stage, the representative will obtain additional medical reports, which further document the disability. However, a very small percentage of cases are reversed at this second level.

Request for Hearing (The Second Appeal)

A claimant who disagrees with the second decision must appeal the second denial by filing a form entitled *Request for a Hearing before an Administrative Law Judge*. There is a strict sixty-day time limit in which to file the Request for a Hearing. Amazingly, the success rate is more than 70% when a claimant is represented at the hearing.

Whether the case is approved with or without a hearing, the claimant is awarded a monthly benefit and receives a check for his or her past-due benefits retroactive to when the initial claim for disability was filed. In some cases, the past-due benefits may go back one year before the claim was filed if the evidence will support a finding that the claimant was disabled as early as one year prior to when the application for Social Security disability was made. In addition, the claimant is entitled to receive insurance benefits (Medicare).

Types of Social Security Programs

There are two types of Social Security disability programs. Depending on your income and assets, you may qualify for both.

Social Security Disability Income

Social Security Disability Income (SSDI) is a program available to those people who have earned work credits prior to becoming disabled. The number of work credits required to qualify depends upon your age when you became disabled. The formula to determine work credits is as follows.

If you were born before 1930, and you became disabled before age 62 in:	You need this many quarters of work credit:
1980	29
1981	30
1982	31
1983	32
1984	33
1985	34
1986	35
1987	36
1988	37
1989	38
1990	39
1991 or later	40

If you were born after 1929, and you became disabled before age:	You need this many quarters of work credit:
42 or younger	20
43	21
44	22
45	23
46	24
47	25
48	26
49	27
50	28
51	29
52	30
53	31
54	32
55	33
56	34
57	35
58	36
59	37
60	38
61	39
62 or older	40

For every three months of work, you earn one work credit. In addition, twenty of the work credits must have been earned within the ten years preceding the date that the claimant became disabled.

As an example, if you were born after 1929 and become disabled at age 46, you would need twenty-four quarters. However, even if you worked continuously since you were 18, but did not work from age 36 to 46, you do not qualify to receive SSDI. Although you have earned seventy-two work credits (18 years times 4 quarters in a year equal 72), you have not earned twenty of those quarters in the last ten years.

When your claim is approved, and you have applied for SSDI, you will receive retroactive benefits, as well as a monthly disability check. The monthly award is calculated based on your past taxable earnings. The monthly award you will receive is the same as if you were 65 and applying for Social Security.

Widow's Benefits

A widow or widower age 50 or older may qualify for Social Security Disability Insurance, providing his or her deceased spouse met the work credit requirements during his or her lifetime. Whether the widow has ever worked is not a factor. This is because the claimant, if found disabled, would be entitled to receive benefits based on the deceased spouse's earnings paid into Social Security. *Widow's benefits* is a gender-neutral term in regards to SSDI.

Supplemental Security Income

People who are found to be disabled and have limited income and assets may be entitled to receive Supplemental Security Income (SSI) payments. Each state varies as to the monthly amount a claimant can receive, as SSI is a program that is funded both by the federal government and the state where the claimant resides. Typically, the monthly amount is about $600. This amount can increase if the claimant has dependent children.

To be eligible to receive SSI, the claimant's monthly resources, or income, cannot exceed an amount set by the state where the claimant resides. For example, in California, a claimant would be ineligible for SSI benefits if he or she is married and his or her spouse earns more than $1,200 per month. The severity of his or her impairment is not considered by the Social Security Administration (SSA). Resources include any income the claimant receives on a monthly basis, including alimony.

PRACTICAL POINT

A claimant cannot have more than $2,000 in property value to receive SSI. If married, the value cannot exceed $3,000. However, Social Security does not consider equity in a home or a car. Therefore, a person can own a $300,000 home and a new car and still qualify to receive SSI.

Under the Social Security regulations, a claimant does not receive benefits for the first five months of disability. Therefore, if it is determined that a claimant was disabled as of July 2006, he or she would not be entitled to receive his or her first benefit check until December 2006.

Veteran's Benefits

In addition to the two programs mentioned, if you are a veteran, you may be eligible for health care services at any of the more than three hundred veterans' health care centers and clinics located throughout the United States.

Depending on your income, you may pay just $15 to see a primary care doctor and $50 to see a specialist. In addition, your medicine could cost no more than $7 per prescription and you may be entitled to dental care. For more information on eligibility, contact the U.S. Department of Veterans Affairs at 800-827-1000 or on the Web at **www.va.gov**.

Survivor's Benefits

If you die, Social Security survivor's benefits can be paid as follows.
  ➤ If your widow or widower is over age 65, he or she can receive 100% of the benefits, and reduced benefits are available at age 60.
  ➤ Your widow or widower can receive benefits at any age if he or she takes care of your child under the age of 16 or is disabled.
  ➤ Your unmarried children under age 18 (or up to age 19, if they are attending school full-time) can receive benefits. Also, if the child is disabled, he or she can get benefits at any age if he or she was disabled before age 22 and remains disabled.
  ➤ If you have been divorced, your former spouse can get benefits under the same circumstances as your widow if your marriage lasted ten years or more. The ten-year rule does not apply if your former spouse is caring for your child under the age of 16, or if the child is disabled and gets benefits.

CHAPTER 20:
THE ROLE
OF AN ATTORNEY

If ever there was an industry that needs a good public relations campaign, it is the law profession. For most people, their first encounter with an attorney is when they have a problem, regardless of whether it was caused by themselves or someone else. Now they have to pay some lawyer to unravel their problem.

The pay for services is often where attorneys run into problems with their clients, as the work that is performed is not apparent. Unlike the pair of shoes you buy at the department store or the milk and eggs purchased at the grocer, you cannot always touch what the attorney does.

For example, you are owed money and retain an attorney to write a letter on your behalf. Your attorney provides you with a copy of the letter prepared and a bill for services, which represents several hours of legal work. The first question you ask yourself is, "How long does it take to write a letter?"

Attorneys bill for their time, and the majority of the work performed by an attorney is completed outside of the client's presence. It includes phone calls and letters to opposing parties and their counsel, research that needs to be completed, and the drive time it takes for the attorney to go to and from court. The meter is running from the minute you give your attorney the green light to proceed. The client is paying for that time based on the attorney's experience and estimate as to how long it will take to complete the matter.

Estate planning attorneys generally perform services based on a fixed fee. Typically, at the initial consultation, the attorney will provide you with the fee for services that will cover all of the work to be performed. It is important that you ask for a written agreement that outlines the work to be prepared and the agreed-upon fee. That way, there can be no confusion as to your financial obligation.

When Do I Need an Attorney?

In general, an attorney should be consulted for any questions that you may have concerning your estate. Though there are excellent self-help books available, the documents that an attorney prepares are designed specifically for you, and they have the attorney's experience and reputation behind them. Therefore, if there was ever a question as to their validity, the attorney could attest that he or she personally prepared them.

More specifically, as discussed in Chapter 13, not everyone needs a Will or a Trust, as state laws differ regarding the size of the estate needed to trigger a probate proceeding. However, you may have questions regarding transferring title to property, liquidating accounts, appointing guardians of your children, and more. Of course, the larger the value of the estate, the greater the chances that there will be tax consequences, for which a tax attorney could best provide advice.

Regardless, even if it is determined that you do not need a Will or a Trust, it is recommended that you have professionally prepared Powers of Attorney for Advance Health and Financial Decisions, as you may have specific needs.

Finding a Lawyer

The best referral source for selecting an attorney is from a friend who had a positive experience with his or her lawyer. In addition, if you have an attorney, but he or she does not practice this type of law, he or she probably knows someone to refer you to. Attorneys are also listed in the phone book Yellow Pages by their specialty in the "Attorney" or "Lawyer" section of the book. The most common subcategories are:

➤ Estate Planning;
➤ Wills and Trusts;
➤ Probate; and,
➤ Elder Law.

In addition, the American Association of Retired Persons (AARP) has networked with attorneys who specialize in estate planning. The attorneys offer reduced fees as well as a free initial consultation. To find an attorney on the AARP network, go to **www.aarp.org**.

Typing the words "estate planning" or "wills and trusts" in your web browser will yield hundreds of websites. You can refine your search by entering your zip code.

Finally, many attorneys who advertise their services will offer a free office consultation. You should inquire when you first contact the attorney if there is a fee for the consultation and ask what the fees are for the services you require. Further, if your situation requires that the attorney's services be performed quickly, ask his or her office staff how long it will take for the work to be completed.

Medicare and Elder Law Issues

If you have issues concerning Medicare benefits or other questions concerning seniors, attorneys who specialize in Elder Law can be a tremendous source for answering your questions. For a listing of Elder Law attorneys in your area, you can visit the National Academy of Elder Law Attorneys at **www.naela.org**. When you click on the icon "Locate an Elder Law Attorney," simply type in your zip code or city and state and a list of attorneys will appear.

CHAPTER 21:
SCAMS

Scam artists prey on people's vulnerabilities. We are most vulnerable during periods of stress and life changes. Seniors in particular are often the targets of consumer fraud, especially after they have lost a loved one. The four most commonly reported scams involve strangers who befriend you, Living Trust seminars, funeral service providers, and identity theft.

New Best Friend Scams

People who live alone, especially when facing health issues, are often susceptible to strangers who befriend them. These strangers run errands, offer transportation to doctor appointments, and perform other acts of generosity. The relationship may begin as innocently as having the door pulled open by a friendly face as you enter your apartment building.

What seems like a good person is really a scammer in disguise. He has taken the first step in winning your trust. As the days and weeks pass, cloaked behind these kind gestures are subtle hints that the acts of these so-called do-gooders come with a price. Initially, your offer to pay for taking you to the doctor is refused, as the scammer says he did it out of the goodness of his heart. Watch out—you are being set up.

Once the scammer has secured your confidence, he will ask for a loan. The scammer will of course pay you back, and with interest. It's just that he has fallen on some hard times, and the money that he was expecting from his parents hasn't come through. You are now dependent on his services and are reluctant to say no. Even worse, you may fear that he could get violent, and you fear for your own safety.

NOTE: While many of the scammers will be male, there are several female scam artists as well. If anyone, male or female, fits this pattern—beware.

This scenario is played out hundreds of times a year in communities across the United States. No one is immune. The key is to recognize the situation. If you feel you may be the target of such a scam, you should share your suspicions with your family or friends. If you have actually given away property under false representations by another, alert the police.

Robert's Story

Robert was living alone in an apartment in Los Angeles. He had a heart condition that caused him to become winded upon any exertion. His son, Josh, lived in Chicago. Though the two talked regularly, the father never told his son about the kind neighbor in the building who often did his food shopping and went to the drugstore to pick up his medicine. He also did not tell his son that he was letting this neighbor deposit his pension check. On a visit to see his dad, Josh offered to pay some bills. Upon comparing Robert's bank statement with his checkbook, Josh discovered that the pension checks had not been deposited and the account balance had been greatly reduced. After Josh questioned his father, the scam became apparent. Josh called the police, who arrested the neighbor for *conversion*, which is wrongfully taking the property of another. It turned out that this person had repeatedly committed similar offenses.

Living Trust Scams

Be especially careful when considering purchasing a Living Trust and other estate planning documents from non-attorneys. Seniors in particular are often targeted by unscrupulous salespeople, who will attempt to sell you a Living Trust regardless of your needs. Each year, thousands of consumers purchase documents they do not need. Worse yet, families face potentially greater costs after the consumer's death, resulting from problems associated with improperly drafted Trusts.

The sales pitch may be very attractive, as they attempt to lure you into buying by making false claims as to what a Trust can and cannot do. (See Chapter 13 for a further discussion of Trusts.) You may be approached in a variety of methods, including:

> ➤ mail solicitations;
> ➤ calls from telemarketers; or,
> ➤ advertisements for "free" seminars and workshops.

Scam artists often will want to meet in your home. They may entice you by offering free documents, such as Living Wills and Powers of Attorney. After they have gained your confidence, they will try to sell you limited partnerships, family partnerships, and limited liability companies. All are supposedly designed to protect your assets, but in reality, they only fatten the wallets of the scam artists.

If a Trust is right for you, an attorney with knowledge of the state law should draft it. The laws that apply to Trusts vary from state to state. Forms, kits, or computer software programs may not be tailored to the requirements of your state. A licensed attorney with expertise in estate planning should prepare, or at least review, your Living Trust. Also, a Trust prepared by an attorney will generally cost less than the price charged by Trust salespeople.

Funeral Industry Scams

Losing a loved one is bad enough, but losing money to unscrupulous funeral home salespeople is outrageous. Although funeral homes are regulated by the Federal Trade Commission, it often becomes a problem of "if you don't ask, they won't tell." That is to say, unless you are prepared with the right questions, you may pay for services that you did not need, such as an expensive casket when the body is being cremated or an embalming fee though there is not going to be a public viewing. Further, similar to any other sales business, funeral homes employ salespeople who work on a commission basis. The more they sell, the more they make!

Harriet's Story

Harriet lost her husband to cancer. After his death, Harriet went with her girlfriend to the funeral home to make arrangements. The funeral director took full advantage of her emotional state of mind by presenting her with very expensive funeral arrangements, including a casket that cost over $5,000. When he finished itemizing all of the other expenses, the total was over $20,000.

Harriet turned to her friend and asked what she thought. Since her friend had never been involved before with funeral costs she signaled that it seemed okay. Harriet then signed the contract, paying one-third of the money owing, with the balance to be billed later.

About a month after the funeral, Harriet contacted me to review the contract, as she was appalled at the costs charged. Her position was that she was too emotional at the time to have closely read the contract and it was unfair for her to be liable for such a great amount.

This argument, however, is very weak if argued in court, as a contract is generally enforceable unless it can be proven that the person signing was acting under the influence of another or was not competent to sign. Though it is correct that the grieving widow was emotional, no one put the pen in her hand and forced her to sign. She could have walked out of the room. In the end, I told Harriet that she was responsible to the funeral home for the unpaid balance, which she was not pleased to hear.

PRACTICAL POINT

Be wary of funeral homes that try to sell you expensive caskets as part of their services. Under the federal Funeral Rule, you may purchase a casket directly instead of being forced to buy from the funeral home, so shop around before committing to a purchase.

For a further discussion of funeral homes and pre-need planning, please refer to Chapters 5 and 6.

Identity Theft Scams

Identity theft has become a major problem for consumers. People who are ill are especially vulnerable, because information about you may be released into the wrong hands. For example, if you are receiving medical treatment at home, you may unwillingly be exposing yourself to identity theft, as others may have access to personal information such as Social Security numbers and bank account information. All of a sudden, you could receive bills for merchandise you never ordered.

To minimize the risk of identity theft, it is important that you have a patient advocate if you cannot make business decisions for yourself. That person becomes your eyes and ears in releasing information to only the parties that require it. Likewise, it is advisable that you are not in your home alone when medical services are being provided. It is very simple for someone to snoop around your important papers while you believe you are receiving medical care.

Lyman's Story

One of the most outrageous acts of identity theft occurred in Seattle. A blood technician drew blood from a patient who had had two bone marrow transplants. Within weeks, Lyman (not his real name) began receiving mail—not from well-wishers, but from banks thanking him for opening up new accounts. This was followed by bills for merchandise he never ordered. As he grew weaker from the chemotherapy, Lyman was unable to pursue the necessary letters and phone calls required to attempt to reverse the damage that was done to his credit. The identity theft consumed all his energy and made it impossible for Lyman to raise money for bone marrow drives for others that he was previously so active in. The perpetrator was eventually sentenced to sixteen months in prison under a new federal law designed to protect patients' privacy.

Health Insurance Scams

With the cost of medical insurance skyrocketing, companies offering very low premiums have been marketing their services to unsuspecting consumers. Too often, however, it is not discovered that the company is bogus until an insurance claim is submitted and then not paid.

Typically, these companies target the self-employed and recently retired through direct marketing and late-night television advertising. The state of Florida, which has seen the greatest share of scam artists preying on the public, has set up a "Verify Before You Buy" 800 phone number so consumers can verify that the company is authorized to sell health insurance. If you have any doubt, contact your state's department of insurance. Remember, if it sounds to good to be true, it probably is.

PRACTICAL POINT
Often, scam insurance companies will use the phrase "like insurance." This is a tip-off that the carrier may not be legitimate.

Other Common Scams

Every day, scam artists find new ways to victimize seniors and those under great stress due to family loss or medical condition. In addition to the scams previously mentioned, some other tricks that scam artists are using include the following.

Financial Advisors and Investment Scams

Beware of investment seminars touting tax shelters. Often, these seminars are selling high-priced insurance products that offer no real tax benefits. It is always prudent to discuss any potential investment with your attorney or tax advisor.

Medicare Fraud

Never give your Medicare number to a stranger. Always check your Medicare statement to verify that you actually received the services charged to Medicare. If you suspect fraud, call Medicare.

Charitable Donations

Watch out for fake charities. Anyone soliciting funds must first register with the state attorney general's office. To find out if a charity has registered, you may contact the attorney general's office or your local Better Business Bureau.

Door-To-Door Solicitation

If someone appears at your door selling a product or service, ask to see a business permit. Regardless, you should resist pressure to buy anything, no matter how tempting the offer or product may appear. Never be too trusting, as appearances can be deceiving.

CHAPTER 22:
WHEN DEATH
IS IMMINENT

The purpose of this book is to provide practical information for you and your loved ones. This chapter addresses the issues your survivors may face upon your passing and the steps to be taken to avoid financial exposure.

Debts of the Deceased

It is a common misbelief that the estate is not responsible for the debts of the decedent. This is not true. If there are assets of the estate, the debts must be paid. A formal probate action does not have to be filed for creditors to begin collection activities.

In the pecking order, creditors of the estate are paid before there can be any distribution to heirs. An exception to this rule is when assets pass directly to named beneficiaries, as in life insurance proceeds, 401(k)s, and IRAs. Also, certain creditors have priority over others—taxes, funeral homes, and health care providers are typically paid before credit card companies.

If probate is required, notices must be sent to all known creditors, putting them on notice to file claims against the estate so they may be paid upon distribution of the assets. They are given a set amount of time to file, and if they do not, they are not paid. Further, a probate notice is published in a newspaper, alerting potential creditors of the estate.

The estate is not legally obligated to pay for debts owed to the creditors if the amounts owed exceed the value of the estate. However, this often does not stop aggressive creditors, who will pursue family members, using intimidating tactics to enforce collection.

Accordingly, it is highly recommended that you take inventory of all of your debts and advise your loved ones of your financial situation.

Following is a Schedule of Debts form that you can fill out and give to your family when death is imminent.

SCHEDULE OF DEBTS

INSTRUCTIONS:

Please list all of your debts that are not paid in full. Under the heading "Type of Debt," describe the type of debt by entering the appropriate letter found in the key section.

KEY:

Automobile and Other Vehicles   (A)
Credit Cards   (C)
Medical   (M)
Real Estate   (R)
Other   (O)

NAME: _____

SSN: _____

Name of Creditor	Account #	Type of Debt	Balance Owed
_____	_____	_____	_____
_____	_____	_____	_____
_____	_____	_____	_____
_____	_____	_____	_____
_____	_____	_____	_____
_____	_____	_____	_____
_____	_____	_____	_____
_____	_____	_____	_____
_____	_____	_____	_____
_____	_____	_____	_____
_____	_____	_____	_____

Notification to Credit Card Companies

Regardless of whether there is a balance owed on an account or the account has been inactive for some time, it is prudent to take inventory of all of your credit card and department store accounts issued in your name. This also applies to accounts in which you and your spouse share an account, and in those situations in which you are a consignor on an account.

Once you have organized the information, a letter should be addressed to your creditors advising them of your situation and requesting that either the account be closed or that your name be removed from the account as an authorized user. The primary reason for this is to prevent unauthorized use of the card that could result in financial exposure to your estate if a creditor were to bring an action against the estate to enforce a debt owed. Remember, even if the estate is not required to file a probate action, it can still be liable for unpaid debts. Accordingly, by sending a letter in advance of your passing, the credit card companies often will, as a matter of public policy, suspend adding interest to the account. Instead, they will work with the representatives of the estate to make payment arrangements.

PRACTICAL POINT
Many credit card companies offer disability insurance as part of their services. This insurance allows payment of your account if you should pass away. At first glance, this may seem like a great idea, as your assets will not be used for payment. However, such policies are very expensive. Proceed cautiously before purchasing this type of insurance.

Likewise, it is important to review your checking and credit card accounts for any automatic withdrawals that you have authorized for payment. For example, Internet providers like AOL may be authorized by you to deduct their monthly fee. Other common examples are newspapers, fitness clubs, and insurance companies.

To prevent these creditors from continued withdrawals, a simple letter that you want to cancel or pay directly is recommended. Even if you leave a nominal balance in your checking account that is insufficient to cover the previously authorized withdrawal, this does not prevent the creditor from trying to collect the monthly fee. Many banks will continue to honor such withdrawals if your account is set up with an overdraft provision. As a result, months could go by after your passing with your estate now responsible for payment to your bank for payments the bank has made.

Miguel's Story

After Miguel passed away, his children listed the house with a realtor and quickly obtained a buyer. Two weeks before the sale was to be completed, I received call from the son. There was a lien on the house placed by a fitness club, of which Miguel was a member. Apparently, the club had not been paid for six months and placed a lien on the residence for $260 plus attorney's fees. Pursuant to the contract that the father had signed, they were within their legal rights to do so. Upon Miguel's passing, the club was never notified and continued to bill for the monthly fee. Though the bank advised the club that there were insufficient funds to cover the automatic checking account withdrawals, the club continued to bill for monthly membership fees. Eventually, the amount owed increased to a point where the account was sent to collection and eventual legal action. All of this could have been prevented if a letter of cancellation had been written.

Notification to Social Security

If you are receiving retirement benefits from Social Security or are disabled and receive benefits through SSI or SSD, the Social Security Administration must be notified as soon as possible upon your passing. Since benefit checks are issued by the third of the month, leave instructions with your loved ones to contact the SSA so to prevent a check from being issued after your passing. The SSA phone number is 800-772-1213. You can also get information on their website, **www.ssa.gov**. In the event a check is issued after death, it cannot be endorsed by the person who had been appointed power of attorney, as the power terminates upon one's passing.

The SSA does provide a one-time death benefit payable only to the spouse of the insured. As of this writing, the amount is $255 and the funds are designed to help defray the costs of burial.

Notification to Disability Insurance and Long-Term Care Insurance Providers

Leave instructions with your loved ones to contact private insurance carriers upon your passing so that benefit checks will not be issued after your passing. The instructions should include the address of the insurance carrier and policy number. Remember, a person previously appointed power of attorney to make financial decisions cannot endorse a check after your passing, as the power of attorney terminates upon death.

Notification to Pension Benefit Providers

If you are married, your spouse may be entitled to receive all or a portion of your pension benefits upon your passing. This may even be applicable if you are divorced. Refer to your pension policy to determine specific benefits. If there is a surviving spouse, instructions with the name, address, and account number should be left for your spouse. In almost all cases, pension benefits pass on to surviving spouses but rarely to children of a pension holder.

Home Maintenance and Other Emergencies

No one knows your home better than you. Part of planning for the inevitable includes having systems in place for when you are no longer here. Therefore, if there were a home emergency, such as a water heater that needed to be replaced, the information that you provided would assist your survivors in arranging the repairs.

A Home Maintenance and Emergency Worksheet to convey this information follows. Use the form to enter the names and phone numbers of companies that you have used for home repairs. There is also a section to include the phone numbers of your utility companies and a section for you to identify where certain equipment is located in your home.

HOME MAINTENANCE AND EMERGENCY WORKSHEET

PROVIDE THE NAME AND PHONE NUMBER FOR EACH OF THE FOLLOWING:

Air Conditioning/Heating _____

Security/Alarm Service Security Code/Password _____

_____

Gate/Apartment Manager _____

Appliance Repair _____

Gardener _____

Pool Service _____

Cleaning Service _____

Plumber _____

Window Cleaning _____

Utility Companies

    Electric _____

    Gas _____

    Phone _____

    Trash _____

    Water _____

Cable/Satellite _____

Newspaper _____

Magazines/Other Publications _____

_____

IN CASE OF AN EMERGENCY, PLEASE IDENTIFY THE LOCATION IN YOUR HOME OF THE FOLLOWING:

Gas Meter _____

Electrical Breaker Panel _____

Sprinkler Control Panel _____

Security Alarm Panel _____

Water Meter _____

Water Shut-Off Valve _____

Air Conditioner _____

Water Heater _____

CHAPTER 23:
UNFINISHED BUSINESS

Receiving news of a terminal illness is devastating. Any plans that you have made are now on hold. What about contracts that you have already entered into or other transactions that will not be completed until after your passing? In planning for the inevitable, this kind of question needs to be addressed to avoid a potential financial hardship for your survivors.

The following list includes the most common type of consumer transactions that might not be completed before your passing:

- ➤ real estate purchases or options to purchase real estate;
- ➤ car, boat, or other vehicle loans or leases;
- ➤ financed purchases of furniture, electronics, and other home furnishings;
- ➤ financed cruise or other vacation packages;
- ➤ the balance of a lease owed on an apartment or house rental;
- ➤ prepaid reservations; and,
- ➤ personal injury, job injury, and other claims or lawsuits in which you are the plaintiff.

Relieving Your Survivors' Burden

When you enter into a contract, to be valid, there must be an agreed time stated for performance. To illustrate, if a car purchase is financed for sixty months at $450 per month, this is known as an installment contract. In the language of the contract, there are provisions if you default or do not pay as per the contract agreement. Such provisions usually include the right of the creditor to call the entire balance due, as well as allow a repossession of the merchandise.

Unless there was a disability insurance policy that was taken out when the contract was signed (see Chapter 18), your estate is liable for the unpaid balance when you pass away. For example, if car payments were not made, the creditor could repossess the vehicle, sell it for its value, and then pursue the estate for any balance still owed on the loan.

To avoid burdening your survivors, it is best to contact your creditors upon learning of a terminal illness to determine if they will agree to cancel the contract. Using the example of a vehicle, a creditor may be inclined to accept return of the vehicle and forgive the balance that may still be owed. This is because the car, if recently purchased or leased, has probably retained its value, and the creditor will be able to sell it for close to what is still owed on the contract.

Unfortunately, this does not usually apply to other items that are financed, such as electronic equipment, as this type of merchandise does not have a high resale value. Therefore, the creditor would be less willing to take back the merchandise.

In the case of a house or apartment rental, the landlord has the right to sue you or your estate for all of the months remaining on the lease. However, he or she also has the duty to mitigate damages—that is, he or she must actively market the property to find a new tenant. Once a new tenant is found, the estate would be liable only for the months that rent was not paid. Again, upon being informed of your health condition, a landlord might consider canceling the lease upon your appeal to reason and release you and your estate from the balance owed on the lease. Rather than make this issue a burden for your survivors, it is best for you to contact your landlord immediately. If he or she is agreeable, make sure that the agreement is in writing and signed by both you and the landlord.

A contract to perform in the future is a binding agreement on both the buyer and the seller. If you enter into a contract but you pass away before the contract is to be performed, your estate can still be held liable if the buyer tries to enforce the terms of the contract.

Samuel's Story

Samuel entered into an agreement to buy a home that he intended to use as a rental for investment purposes. He put down $25,000 as a deposit and the deal was to close in seventy-five days. Shortly thereafter, he was diagnosed with an aggressive form of lung cancer. Samuel passed away before the close of escrow, and the owner of the real estate successfully sued the estate for what is known as *specific performance*. The legal theory was that the parties had entered into a specific agreement and, through no fault of the seller, the buyer did not perform. As a result, the estate was ordered to complete the sale.

Prepaid Purchases

Everyone likes getting a good deal. When you can save money, it is not uncommon to pay for something in full before you intend to use it. The best example is airline tickets. The major airlines always advertise airfare sales wherein you can purchase your tickets now for travel in the future. As long as the ticket is paid in full, the price is locked in. The problem occurs if, because of an illness, you will not be able to use the tickets for which you have paid.

Depending on the contract, there is language that explains whether the purchase is nonrefundable or if a penalty or forfeiture of part of the purchase price is applied for cancellation. Airline tickets are generally nonrefundable, but can be reissued after payment of a reissuance fee. The best approach, however, is to contact customer service regardless of how the contract may read. Insist on speaking to a manager to explain your situation. Some people have successfully had a return of their money upon presentation of medical documentation. This especially applies if the tickets have been recently purchased.

Personal Injury and Other Legal Actions

If you have a claim against someone who caused injuries to you, your heirs cannot pursue the claim unless the injuries were the reason for your passing. To illustrate, if you had an automobile accident in which you were injured, and the case had not settled, your passing extinguishes the claim. The only exception is if your injuries caused your death. In that case, your surviving family members can continue the claim as a wrongful death action. The same applies if you had a job injury.

For all other legal matters, the language of the contract that you may be suing under will dictate whether or not your heirs can pursue your claim. Most contracts include language that states that "any claim inures to the benefit of the heirs." That is, your heirs can continue to pursue the claim on behalf of your estate. If an attorney represents you, you should consult with him or her concerning this issue.

Copyrights, Patents, and Trademarks

Intellectual property is property that you may have written or designed. If you are the owner of such property and it has been protected legally by a copyright, for example, the rights to the property belong to your estate after your passing. The Personal Data and Record Locator found on page 129 has space to insert the location of such documents.

CONCLUSION

Planning for the time when you are no longer here is not a pleasant task. Just the thought of someday not being with your loved ones is overwhelming. However, if you have led your life in an organized manner, there is no reason why that pattern should not continue as you consider end-of-life decisions. If you have always taken the "I'll do it tomorrow" approach, consider that tomorrow may be here sooner than you think.

Now is the time to take charge. Planning for the inevitable does not mean that you have to wait for a serious or life-threatening illness before you make your wishes known. Now is the time to have thoughtful and serious conversations with your loved ones and friends so they know your wishes.

My Wishes was written to explore all of the issues one faces at the end of life, including both personal needs and legal consequences. Likewise, as a gift to your survivors, the information provided will greatly reduce their uncertainty by knowing what you wanted, and will help prevent both the financial and psychological burdens that often become the responsibilities of the survivors.

I hope that you found the checklists and forms for systematically organizing your assets and other important documents helpful. My hope is that when you read the material, you maintained an ongoing conversation with yourself as you planned your wishes. Refer to your conscience and always use your own judgment as the ultimate decider. You need to feel confident that you made the right decisions.

Finally, *My Wishes* is intended to give you peace of mind. It will provide you comfort in knowing that a plan is in place if a tragedy should occur. You owe it to yourself and your loved ones to be prepared.

GLOSSARY

A

advance directive. A document authorized by statutes in all states, in which a person appoints someone as his or her proxy or representative to make decisions on maintaining extraordinary life support if the person becomes too ill, is in a coma, or is certain to die. In most states, the basic language has been developed by medical associations or other experts, and may provide various choices as to when such maintenance of life can be terminated. The decision must be made in consultation with the patient's doctor. The advance directive permits a terminal patient to die with dignity and protects the physician or hospital from liability for withdrawing or limiting life support.

anatomical gift. Another way of saying that you wish to donate some or all of your organs after you pass away. This term is usually found in advance health care directives as well as living wills.

B

beneficiary. Any person or entity (like a charity) that is to receive assets or profits from an estate, a trust, an insurance policy, or any instrument in which there is distribution.

C

conservator. A person, official, or institution designated to take over and protect the interests of a person who is no longer competent to make decisions for him- or herself.

D

durable power of attorney. A written document signed by a person giving another person the power to act in conducting the signer's business, including signing papers, checks, title documents, and contracts; handling bank accounts; and other financial activities, in the name of the person granting the power. The person receiving the power of attorney (the agent) is the attorney in fact for the person giving the power. A power of attorney may expire on a date stated in the document or upon written cancellation. Regardless, it automatically expires upon death. Usually, the signer acknowledges before a notary public that he or she executed the power, so that it is recordable if necessary, as in a real estate transaction.

E

estate. The assets and liabilities left by a person at death.

eulogy. A written tribute or speech that is given to commemorate someone who has passed away. A eulogy usually flatters and showcases the life of the decedent.

executor. The person appointed to administer the estate of a person who has died leaving a will that nominates that person. Unless there is a valid objection, the judge will appoint the person named in the will to be executor. The executor must ensure that the person's desires expressed in the will are carried out. Practical responsibilities include gathering up and protecting the assets of the estate; obtaining information in regard to all

beneficiaries named in the will and any other potential heirs; collecting and arranging for payment of debts of the estate; approving or disapproving creditor's claims; making sure estate taxes are calculated, forms filed, and tax payments made; and in all ways assisting the attorney for the estate.

G

gift. The voluntary transfer of property or money to another person, completely free of payment or strings, while both the giver and the recipient are still alive. Large gifts are subject to the federal gift tax, and in some states, to a state gift tax. As with all tax questions, professional assistance in gift tax planning is vital.

guardian. Someone who is entrusted with the care of the children or property of another.

H

health care power of attorney. A document that allows an individual to appoint someone else to make health care decisions for his or her medical care if he or she is unable to make those decisions. This document is also known as an advance directive.

heir. One who inherits or is entitled to inherit property.

holographic will. A will entirely handwritten, dated, and signed by the testator, but not signed by required witnesses. Under those conditions, it is valid in about half the states, despite the lack of witnesses. A letter that has all the elements of a will may be a holographic will.

hospice. A program in which a person diagnosed with a terminal illness can get support, as well as nursing or medical care. Usually for those with a limited time to live, hospice emphasizes dying at home in a supportive and loving atmosphere.

I

inter vivos trust. *See living trust.*

L

last will and testament. A fancy and redundant way of saying "will." Lawyers and clients like the formal resonance of the language. A document will be the "last" will if the maker of it dies before writing another one.

living will. A document in which the signer requests to be allowed to die rather than be kept alive by artificial means, if disabled beyond a reasonable expectation of recovery.

living trust. A trust created during the trustor's lifetime. A living trust should not be confused with a living will, which provides for medical care decisions when a person is terminally ill.

P

probate. The process of proving that a will is valid, and thereafter administering the estate of a dead person according to the terms of the will. The first step is to file the purported will with the clerk of the appropriate court in the county where the deceased person lived, along with a petition to have the court approve the will and appoint the executor named in the will (or if none is available, an administrator) with a declaration of a person who had signed the will as a witness. If the court determines the will is valid, the court then admits the will to probate.

T

testamentary trust. A trust, created by a will, that only comes into effect upon the death of the person who wrote the will.

testator. The creator of a will.

trust. An instrument by which one person or entity holds legal title to property designated by the trust for the benefit of another.

trustee. A person or entity who holds the assets of a trust for the benefit of the beneficiaries, and manages the trust and its assets under the terms stated in the trust that created it. In many living trusts, the creator of the trust names him- or herself (or themselves) as the original trustee who will manage the trust until his or her death, when it is taken over by a successor trustee. If a trustee has title to property, it is held only for the benefit of the trust and its beneficiaries.

trustor. The creator of a trust.

W

will. A written document that leaves the estate of the person who signed the will to named persons or entities (beneficiaries), including portions or percentages of the estate, specific gifts, creation of trusts for management, and future distribution of all or a portion of the estate (a testamentary trust). A will usually names an executor to manage the estate, states the authority and obligations of the executor in the management and distribution of the estate, sometimes gives funeral and burial instructions, nominates guardians of minor children, and spells out other terms. To be valid, the will must be signed by the testator, dated, and witnessed by two people (except in Vermont, which requires three witnesses). A signed and dated will totally in the handwriting of the testator, but without witnesses, is valid in many, but not all, states. If the will (also called a last will and testament) is still in force at the time of the death of the testator, and there is a substantial estate or real estate, then the will must be probated (approved by the court, and managed and distributed by the executor under court supervision).

will contest. A lawsuit challenging the validity of a will or its terms. Bases for contesting a will include the competency of the maker of the will at the time the will was signed, the undue influence of someone who used pressure to force the testator to give him or her substantial gifts in the will, the existence of another will or trust, and illegal terms or technical faults in the execution of the will, such as not having been validly witnessed. A trial of the will contest must be held before the will can be probated, since if the will is invalid, it cannot be probated.

APPENDIX:
BLANK FORMS

Photocopy and fill out the following forms as part of your preparations. Refer to the text of the book for instructions on what information to include.

Table of Forms

RECORDING YOUR PLANS
FOR ADVANCE HEALTH CARE PLANNING

An advance health care plan states your wishes for medical care. It is a guide for others who may need to make decisions on your behalf. Be aware that the decisions you make can always be changed. Further, you can entirely disregard any previously made health care plans by destroying this document. However, if you have provided copies of this form to anyone, you will need to notify them of any changes or of the destruction of this form.

WORKSHEET

1. If I were dying, I would request the following approach to treatment. (If I chose more than one, I have shown the order of preference.)

❏ My main wish would be for care that allows me to be comfortable, peaceful, and free from pain (including hospice care if possible).

❏ I would want to go to the hospital for some treatment if needed for comfort, but I would not want to be connected to life support machines.

❏ If it were unclear whether a life support treatment would improve my chances of living, I would like to have a brief period of treatment in the hospital, but would like the treatment stopped if I did not improve.

❏ I would like life support treatments to prolong my life as long as possible, even if those treatments made me uncomfortable.

❏ I would like to donate organs or tissues and would like life support treatments if needed for organ donation.

❏ Other _____

_____

2. If I were dying and were unable to eat, I would want the following treatments.

❏ I would want to have a tube inserted into my stomach, nose, or mouth to feed me if I could not eat.

❏ I would not want a feeding tube if I could not eat.

3. Following my death, I would want to be an organ, eye, and/or tissue donor.
Yes _____ No _____

4. When I am dying, please keep me as comfortable as possible. Here are some guidelines. (Check the items below that express your wishes. Make notes to personalize these items as you wish.)

❏ Please give me adequate medication to relieve pain, shortness of breath, or other distressing symptoms.

❏ I prefer that enough pain medication be given to me to keep me comfortable, even if this means I am not fully aware of what is going on.

❏ I prefer that I be medicated for pain, but I also want to be aware of my surroundings and what is going on. I understand this may mean my pain control may not be complete.

❏ I wish to have other non-medicine measures taken to help me be comfortable.

❏ Please provide all measures to keep me fresh and clean (baths or sponging, regular mouth care, other personal hygiene, clean linens, back rubs, massage, healing touch, turning, repositioning, and so on).

5. The following will also bring me peace and comfort.

❏ Music (specify type) _____

❏ Readings (specify) _____

❏ Prayers (specify) _____

6. In addition to my family, I wish to have the support of the following person(s).

_____

_____

7. I do not wish to be visited by the following person(s).

_____

_____

Dated: _____

_____
PRINT YOUR NAME

_____
SIGN YOUR NAME

FUNERAL SERVICE PLANNER

Tell your survivors that you filled out this planner. If you do not want to discuss its contents, make sure to inform your loved ones where it may be located.

YOUR NAME: _____

1. FUNERAL HOME

I would like the following funeral home to handle my final wishes.

Name: _____

Phone Number: _____

Address: _____

2. CASKET

Use this space to describe the type of casket (material, color, etc.) you would like. If you already have a model in mind, say so here. This space can also be used to tell your family about the funeral home of your choice and your wishes for the amount of money you would like to spend. Be as descriptive as you would like.

_____

_____

_____

_____

Open _____ or Closed _____ Casket

3. SERVICE

I would like a service: _____ Yes _____ No

If yes, I want a traditional burial service: _____ Yes _____ No

If so, I would like it held at:

House of Worship (insert name) _____

Chapel or Funeral Home (insert name) _____

Graveside Only _____

If I selected something other than graveside only, I would like a graveside service as well: _____ Yes _____ No

4. TYPE OF SERVICE

Religious _____   Personalized _____   Military _____

I would like a memorial service: _____ Yes _____ No

I would like a viewing or visitation: _____ Yes _____ No

5. FLOWERS

The following are the types of flowers I would like at my service.

_____

_____

6. STATIONERY

I would like the following stationery available at my service (i.e., memorial cards, thank you cards, prayer cards).

_____

7. MUSIC

I would like the following music to be played.

During visitation: _____

During the service: _____

Hymns for the service: _____

Soloist: _____

8. PALLBEARERS

1. _____
2. _____
3. _____
4. _____
5. _____
6. _____
7. _____ (as an alternate)
8. _____ (as an alternate)
9. _____ (as an alternate)

9. CLERGY

I would like the following person to officiate my service.

_____

10. CEMETERY/FINAL RESTING PLACE

If you have already purchased a plot or a space has been reserved for you in a family plot, please enter that information here. If you have not made pre-need arrangements, but have a place in mind, add your wishes here.

_____

_____

_____

11. EULOGY/SPEAKERS

I would like the following person/persons to speak at my service.

_____

_____

_____

12. MONUMENTS

Use this area to describe the type of monument or headstone you would like. If you have already decided on the inscription, provide that information.

_____

_____

_____

13. MISCELLANEOUS

Use this space to add anything that is not covered in this planner.

_____

_____

_____

_____

_____

OBITUARY WORKSHEET

YOUR FULL LEGAL NAME *(nickname may be included in parentheses)*

_____

CITY OR TOWN OF RESIDENCE _____

DATE OF BIRTH _____

PLACE OF BIRTH _____

SURVIVED BY LIST *(Insert names of living relatives)*

Spouse _____

Parents _____

_____

Children _____

_____

Sisters _____

_____

Brothers _____

_____

Grandchildren and Great-Grandchildren (insert numbers of) _____

Predeceased by (spouse, child, parent, sibling) _____

_____

EDUCATION/DEGREES

_____

_____

WORK HISTORY

_____

_____

OPTIONAL INFORMATION *(special interests or hobbies)*

_____

_____

ASSOCIATIONS *(membership in local or national organizations)*

_____

_____

SPECIAL AFFILIATIONS/VOLUNTEER WORK

_____

_____

MILITARY SERVICE

_____

_____

OTHER

_____

_____

WILL PREPARATION WORKSHEET

I. YOUR ESTATE

List the contents of your estate, including bank accounts, stocks, 401(k)s, IRAs, real estate, motor vehicles, life insurance, and anything else that you may own, whether by yourself or with another person. For this purpose, an estimate of the value is sufficient.

Bank Accounts

1. _____
2. _____
3. _____
4. _____

Stocks, Bonds, Treasury Notes, Other Investments

1. _____
2. _____
3. _____
4. _____

Life Insurance, IRAs, Pension, 401(k)

1. _____
2. _____
3. _____
4. _____

Real Estate (address)

1. _____
2. _____

Tangible Personal Property

(This category includes furniture, jewelry, and artwork—anything of significant value or that you would like to go to a particular person.)

1. _____
2. _____
3. _____
4. _____

II. BENEFICIARIES

List the people you would like to receive a part of your estate, including family members, friends, and charities. As you transfer this information to your will in the "Bequests" section, determine what percentage or specific item each person should receive. Typically, you would leave your entire estate to your spouse, except for bequests of specific items to others. If your spouse has predeceased you, divide your estate equally among your children.

Spouse _____

Children

1. _____
2. _____
3. _____
4. _____

Other Individuals
(Include friends, grandchildren, brothers, sisters, or anyone else to whom you would like to give a part of your estate.)

1. _____
2. _____
3. _____
4. _____

Charities
(List any religious or other nonprofit organizations to which you would like to make a bequest. This may reduce the taxes on your estate.)

1. _____
2. _____
3. _____
4. _____

III. EXECUTOR

Name the person or persons you would like to appoint to administer your estate. He or she will carry out your wishes as stated in your will. Also name an alternate in case the first person appointed cannot serve for any reason.

Executor _____

Alternate _____

IV. GUARDIAN OF CHILDREN

The most important purpose of a will for most younger people is the appointment of a guardian for their children under age 18. Also name an alternate in case the first person appointed cannot serve for any reason.

Guardian _____

Alternate _____

LAST WILL AND TESTAMENT
OF

_____

I, _____, a resident of _____ County, state of _____, declare this to be my Will and I hereby revoke all Wills and Codicils previously made by me.

FIRST: Family Status:

I declare that I am married to _____ and I have _____ children from this marriage, namely, _____, _____, _____.

SECOND: Appointment of Executor:

I appoint _____ as Executor of this Will, to serve without bond. If the person named shall have predeceased me or should for any reason be unable or unwilling to serve as Executor, I appoint _____ as Executor of this Will, to serve without bond.

THIRD: Executor's Power:

I authorize my Executor to sell, at either public or private sale, any property belonging to my estate, either with or without notice, subject only to such confirmation as may be required by law, and to hold, manage, and operate any such property.

FOURTH: Non-Exercise of Power of Appointment:

I hereby refrain from exercising any testamentary power of appointment that I may have at the time of my death.

FIFTH: Taxes:

My Executor shall pay from the residue of my estate all inheritance, estate, and other death taxes (excluding any additional tax that may be assessed under Internal Revenue Code Section 2032[a], including interest and penalties, that may, because of my death, be attributable to any assets properly inventoried in my probate estate). The taxes shall be charged against my estate as though they were ordinary expenses of administration without adjustment among the beneficiaries of my Will.

SIXTH: Bequests:

I give, devise, and bequeath my entire estate as follows:

A.

B.

SEVENTH: Non-Contest:

Except as otherwise provided in this Will, I have intentionally and with full knowledge omitted to provide for heirs. If any beneficiary under this Will in any manner, directly or indirectly, contests this Will or any part of its provisions, any share or interest in my estate given to that contesting beneficiary under this Will is revoked and shall be disposed of in the same manner provided herein as if that contesting beneficiary had predeceased me without issue.

EIGHTH: <u>Definitions</u>:

For the purpose of construing the terms of this Will:

A. Except when the context of this Will requires otherwise, the singular includes the plural, and the masculine gender includes the feminine and neuter.

B. The terms "issue," "child," and "children" include a person born out of wedlock if a parent-child relationship exists between this person and one through whom this person claims benefits under this Will. These terms do not include persons who are adults at the time of adoption.

C. For purposes of this Will, any beneficiary who dies within sixty (60) days after my death shall be deemed to have died before me.

Executed this _____ day of _____, 200_____ at _____, state of _____.

_____
Name

On this date, _____ signed this document and declared it to be his/her LAST WILL in our presence, and in the presence of each other, signed as witnesses below. Each of us observed the signing of this Will by him/her and by each other subscribing witness and knows that each signature is the true signature of the person whose name was signed.

Each of us is a competent witness. We are acquainted with him/her and attest that he/she is now more than eighteen (18) years of age. To the best of our knowledge, he/she is of sound mind at this time and is not acting under duress, menace, fraud, misrepresentation or undue influence.

Each of us declares under penalty of perjury that the foregoing statement is true and correct, and that each of us signed below on this _____ day of _____, 200___, at _____, state of _____.

Signature: _____

Print Name: _____

Address: _____

_____

Signature: _____

Print Name: _____

Address: _____

_____

LAST WILL AND TESTAMENT
OF

_____

I, _____, a resident of _____ County, state of _____, declare this to be my Will and I hereby revoke all Wills and Codicils previously made by me.

FIRST: <u>Family Status:</u>
I declare that I am married to _____ and that I have _____ child/children by this marriage namely, _____, _____, and _____.

SECOND: <u>Appointment of Executor:</u>
I appoint _____ as Executor of this Will, to serve without bond. If the person named shall have predeceased me or should for any reason be unable or unwilling to serve as Executor, I appoint _____ as Executor of this Will, to serve without bond.

THIRD: <u>Executor's Power:</u>
I authorize my Executor to sell, at either public or private sale, any property belonging to my estate, either with or without notice, subject only to such confirmation as may be required by law, and to hold, manage, and operate any such property.

FOURTH: <u>Nomination of Guardian:</u>
If my child/children are minors at the time of my death, and my spouse has predeceased me, then I hereby nominate _____ as Guardian of my child/children. If the Guardian named declines or is unable to act, or after appointment ceases to act as Guardian, then I do nominate _____ as Guardian of my child/children.

FIFTH: <u>Non-Exercise of Power of Appointment:</u>
I hereby refrain from exercising any testamentary power of appointment that I may have at the time of my death.

SIXTH: <u>Taxes:</u>
My Executor shall pay from the residue of my estate all inheritance, estate, and other death taxes (excluding any additional tax that may be assessed under Internal Revenue Code Section 2032[a], including interest and penalties, that may, because of my death, be attributable to any assets properly inventoried in my probate estate). The taxes shall be charged against my estate as though they were ordinary expenses of administration without adjustment among the beneficiaries of my Will.

SEVENTH: <u>Bequests:</u>
I give, devise, and bequeath my entire estate as follows:

A.

B.

EIGHTH: <u>Non-Contest:</u>

Except as otherwise provided in this Will, I have intentionally and with full knowledge omitted to provide for heirs. If any beneficiary under this Will in any manner, directly or indirectly, contests this Will or any part of its provisions, any share or interest in my estate given to that contesting beneficiary under this Will is revoked and shall be disposed of in the same manner provided herein as if that contesting beneficiary had predeceased me without issue.

NINTH: <u>Definitions:</u>

For the purpose of construing the terms of this Will:

A. Except when the context of this Will requires otherwise, the singular includes the plural, and the masculine gender includes the feminine and neuter.

B. The terms "issue," "child," and "children" include a person born out of wedlock if a parent-child relationship exists between this person and one through whom this person claims benefits under this Will. These terms do not include persons who are adults at the time of adoption.

C. For purposes of this will, any beneficiary who dies within sixty (60) days after my death shall be deemed to have died before me.

Executed this _____ day of _____, 200_____ at _____,
state of _____.

_____
Name

On this date, _____ signed this document and declared it to be his/her LAST WILL in our presence, and in the presence of each other, signed as witnesses below. Each of us observed the signing of this Will by him/her and by each other subscribing witness and knows that each signature is the true signature of the person whose name was signed.

Each of us is a competent witness. We are acquainted with him/her and attest that he/she is now more than eighteen (18) years of age. To the best of our knowledge, he/she is of sound mind at this time and is not acting under duress, menace, fraud, misrepresentation or undue influence.

Each of us declares under penalty of perjury that the foregoing statement is true and correct, and that each of us signed below on this _____ day of _____, 200____, at _____, state of _____.

Signature: _____
Print Name: _____
Address: _____
_____

Signature: _____
Print Name: _____
Address: _____
_____

FAMILY MEDICAL HISTORY AND
HEALTH INSURANCE INFORMATION

Your child's name _____

List any known allergies (food, medicine, other) _____

_____

Physician's name, address, phone number _____

_____

_____

Your child's name _____

List any known allergies (food, medicine, other) _____

_____

Physician's name, address, phone number _____

_____

_____

Your child's name _____

List any known allergies (food, medicine, other) _____

_____

Physician's name, address, phone number _____

_____

_____

Name of health insurance company _____

Policy/group number _____

Claims phone number _____

Location of immunization records _____

Additional information _____

_____

_____

_____

PERSONAL MEDICAL HISTORY

Questions could arise concerning diseases or illnesses that might have a link to family history. This information could be useful should a child or other closely related family member become sick. To pass on your medical history information, a personal health history worksheet should be completed. Following is a sample that you can use, with space at the end to note illnesses or conditions that other family members had.

NAME OF PRIMARY PHYSICIAN:

_____

Phone Number: _____

Address: _____

PLEASE CIRCLE EACH MEDICAL CONDITION THAT YOU HAVE EVER BEEN TREATED FOR:

Alcoholism

Alzheimer's disease

Anemia/hemophilia

Cancer/leukemia/benign tumors

Circulatory problems

Crippling arthritis

Depression

Diabetes—child/adult

Digestive disorders/colitis/ulcers

Heart disorders

High blood pressure

High cholesterol

Kidney disorders

Lung problems/asthma

Mental illness

Muscular disorders/muscular dystrophy/multiple sclerosis

Nervous disorders/convulsions/seizures

Parkinson's disease

Stroke

Vision problems/glaucoma

Other (specify) _____

Other (specify) _____

Other (specify) _____

If you have any known allergies (food, medicine, plant, other), please list them:

_____

_____

Please use these lines to list names of family members who had any of the above conditions, and which conditions they had:

_____

_____

_____

LIVING WILL (A DIRECTIVE TO MY PHYSICIAN)

I, _____, being of sound mind, willfully and voluntarily make known my desire that my dying not be artificially prolonged under the circumstances set forth below, and declare that:

If at any time I should have an incurable injury, disease, or illness certified to be a terminal condition by two physicians who have personally examined me, one of whom is my attending physician, and the physicians have determined that my death will occur unless life-sustaining procedures are used, and if the application of life-sustaining procedures would serve only to artificially prolong the dying process, I direct that life-sustaining procedures be withheld or withdrawn and that I be permitted to die naturally and with only the performance of medical procedures deemed necessary to provide me with comfort and care.

I further direct that if at any time I should be in a permanent vegetative state or an irreversible coma as certified by two physicians who have personally examined me, one of whom is my attending physician, and the physicians have determined that the application of life-sustaining procedures, including artificially administered food and fluid, will only artificially prolong my life in a permanent vegetative state or irreversible coma, I direct that these procedures, including the administration of food or fluids, be withheld or withdrawn, and that I be permitted to die naturally with only the administration of medication to alleviate pain or the performance of medical procedures necessary to provide me with comfort and care.

In the absence of my ability to give directions regarding the use of life-sustaining procedures, it is my intention that this Declaration be honored by my family and attending physician as the final expression of my legal right to refuse medical or surgical treatment and accept the consequences of such refusal.

I understand the full import of this Declaration, and I have emotional and mental capacity to make this declaration.

Dated: _____

_____ Signature

State of _____

County of _____

On this _____ day of _____, 200____, before me, _____, a notary public in and for said county and state, residing herein, duly commissioned and sworn, personally appeared _____, personally known to me (or proved to me on the basis of satisfactory evidence) to be the person whose name is subscribed to the within instrument and acknowledged to me that he/she executed the same in his/her authorized capacity, and that by his/her signature on the instrument the person, or entity upon behalf of which the person acted, executed the instrument.

WITNESS my hand and official seal.

_____

Notary Public

EXPLANATION

You have the right to give instructions about your own health care. You also have the right to name someone else to make health care decisions for you. This form lets you do either or both of these things. It also lets you express your wishes regarding donation of organs and the designation of your primary physician.

Part 1 of this form is a power of attorney for health care. Part 1 lets you name another individual as agent to make health care decisions for you if you become incapable of making your own decisions, or if you want someone else to make those decisions for you now even though you are still capable. You may also name an alternate agent to act for you if your first choice is not willing, able, or reasonably available to make decisions for you. (Your agent may not be an operator or employee of a community care facility or a residential care facility where you are receiving care, or your supervising health care provider or employee of the health care institution where you are receiving care, unless your agent is related to you or is a coworker.)

Unless the form you sign limits the authority of your agent, your agent may make all health care decisions for you. This form has a place for you to limit the authority of your agent. You need not limit the authority of your agent if you wish to rely on your agent for all health care decisions that may have to be made. If you choose not to limit the authority of your agent, your agent will have the right to:

a. Consent or refuse consent to any care, treatment, service, or procedure to maintain, diagnose, or otherwise affect a physical or mental condition.

b. Select or discharge health care providers and institutions.

c. Approve or disapprove diagnostic tests, surgical procedures, and programs of medication.

d. Direct the provision, withholding, or withdrawal of artificial nutrition and hydration, and all other forms of health care, including cardiopulmonary resuscitation.

e. Make anatomical gifts, authorize an autopsy, and direct disposition of remains.

Part 2 of this form lets you give specific instructions about any aspect of your health care, whether or not you appoint an agent. Choices are provided for you to express your wishes regarding the provision, withholding, or withdrawal of treatment to keep you alive, as well as the provision of pain relief. Space is also provided for you to add to the choices you have made or for you to write out any additional wishes. If you are satisfied to allow your agent to determine what is best for you in making end-of-life decisions, you need not fill out Part 2 of this form.

Part 3 of this form lets you express an intention to donate your bodily organs and tissues following your death.

Part 4 of this form lets you designate a physician to have primary responsibility for your health care.

After completing this form, sign and date the form at the end.

The form must be signed by two qualified witnesses or acknowledged before a notary public. Give a copy of the signed and completed form to your physician, to any other health care providers you may have, to any health care institution at which you are receiving care, and to any health care agents you have named. You should talk to the person you have named as agent to make sure that he or she understands your wishes and is willing to take the responsibility.

You have the right to revoke this advance health care directive or replace this form at any time.

POWER OF ATTORNEY FOR HEALTH CARE

PART 1

(1.1) **DESIGNATION OF AGENT:** I, _____, presently a resident of _____ County, state of _____, designate the following individual as my agent to make health care decisions for me: _____, presently a resident of _____ County, state of _____.

(1.1a) If I revoke my agent's authority or if my agent is not willing, able, or reasonably available to make a health care decision for me, I designate as my first alternate agent _____, presently a resident of _____ County, state of _____.

(1.2) **AGENT'S AUTHORITY:** My agent is authorized to make all health care decisions for me, including decisions to provide, withhold, or withdraw artificial nutrition and hydration and all other forms of health care to keep me alive, except as I state here:

_____

_____

_____

(Add additional sheets if needed.)

(1.3) **WHEN AGENT'S AUTHORITY BECOMES EFFECTIVE:** My agent's authority to make health care decisions for me takes effect immediately.

(1.4) **AGENT'S OBLIGATION:** My agent shall make health care decisions for me in accordance with this power of attorney for health care, any instructions I give in Part 2 of this form, and my other wishes to the extent known to my agent. To the extent my wishes are unknown, my agent shall make health care decisions for me in accordance with what my agent determines to be in my best interest. In determining my best interest, my agent shall consider my personal values to the extent known to my agent.

(1.5) **AGENT'S POST-DEATH AUTHORITY:** My agent is authorized to make anatomical gifts, authorize an autopsy, and direct disposition of my remains, except as I state here or in Part 3 of this form.

_____

_____

_____

(Add additional sheets if needed.)

(1.6) **NOMINATION OF CONSERVATOR:** If a conservator of my person needs to be appointed for me by a court, I nominate the agent designated in this form. If that agent is not willing, able, or reasonably available to act as conservator, I nominate the alternate agents whom I have named, in the order designated.

PART 2
INSTRUCTIONS FOR HEALTH CARE

If you fill out this part of the form, you may strike any wording you do not want.

(2.1) **END-OF-LIFE DECISIONS:** I direct that my health care providers and others involved in my care provide, withhold, or withdraw treatment in accordance with the choice I have initialed below:

_____(a) Choice Not To Prolong Life. I do not want my life to be prolonged if (1) I have an incurable and irreversible condition that will result in my death within a relatively short time, (2) I become unconscious and, to a reasonable degree of medical certainty, I will not regain consciousness, or (3) the likely risks and burdens of treatment would outweigh the expected benefits, OR

_____(b) Choice To Prolong Life. I want my life to be prolonged as long as possible within the limits of generally accepted health care standards.

(2.2) **RELIEF FROM PAIN:** Except as I state in the following space, I direct that treatment for alleviation of pain or discomfort be provided at all times, even if it hastens my death:

_____

_____

_____

(Add additional sheets if needed.)

(2.3) **OTHER WISHES:** (If you do not agree with any of the optional choices above and wish to write your own, or if you wish to add to the instructions you have given above, you may do so here.) I direct that:

_____

_____

_____

(Add additional sheets if needed.)

PART 3
DONATION OF ORGANS AT DEATH
(OPTIONAL)

(3.1) Upon my death (initial applicable):

_____(a) I give any needed organs, tissues, or parts, OR

_____(b) I give the following organs, tissues, or parts:

_____

_____

_____ OR

_____(c) My gift is for the following purposes (strike out any of the following you do **not** want):

     (1) Transplant

     (2) Therapy

     (3) Research

     (4) Education

_____(d) I do not wish to donate my organs.

PART 4
PRIMARY PHYSICIAN
(OPTIONAL)

(4.1) I designate the following physician as my primary physician:

_____
(name of physician)

_____
(address)   (city)   (state)   (zip)

_____
(phone)

OPTIONAL: If the physician I have designated above is not willing, able, or reasonably available to act as my primary physician, I designate the following physician as my primary physician:

_____
(name of physician)

_____
(address)   (city)   (state)   (zip)

_____
(phone)

PART 5

(5.1) **EFFECT OF COPY:** A copy of this form has the same effect as the original.

(5.2) **SIGNATURE:** Sign and date the form here:

_____

Date _____

(5.3) **STATEMENT OF WITNESSES:** We declare under penalty of perjury under the laws of _____ (1) that the individual who signed or acknowledged this advance health care directive is personally known to me, or that the individual's identity was proven to me by convincing evidence, (2) that the individual signed or acknowledged this advance directive in my presence, (3) that the individual appears to be of sound mind and under no duress, fraud, or undue influence, (4) that I am not a person appointed as agent by this advance directive, and (5) that I am not the individual's health care provider, an employee of the individual's health care provider, the operator of a community care facility, an employee of an operator of a community care facility, the operator of a residential care facility for the elderly, or an employee of an operator of a residential care facility for the elderly.

Print Name: _____

Signature: _____

Address: _____

Dated: _____

Print Name: _____

Signature: _____

Address: _____

Dated: _____

(5.4) **ADDITIONAL STATEMENT OF WITNESSES:** At least one of the above witnesses must also sign the following declaration. I further declare under penalty of perjury under the laws of the state of _____ that I am not related to the individual executing this advance health care directive by blood, marriage, or adoption, and to the best of my knowledge, I am not entitled to any part of the individual's Estate upon his or her death under a Will now existing or by operation of law.

_____

(signature of witness)

(5.5) STATE OF _____   )
       COUNTY OF _____   )

On this _____ day of _____, 20_____ before me, a notary public in and for said county and state, residing herein, duly commissioned and sworn, personally appeared _____, personally known to me (or proved to me on the basis of satisfactory evidence) to be the person whose name is subscribed to the within instrument and acknowledged to me that he/she executed the same in his/her authorized capacity, and that by his/her signature on the instrument the person, or entity upon behalf of which the person acted, executed the instrument.

WITNESS my hand and official seal.

_____

(Signature of Notary Public)

DURABLE POWER OF ATTORNEY

WARNING TO PERSON EXECUTING THIS DOCUMENT:

THIS IS AN IMPORTANT LEGAL DOCUMENT. IT CREATES A DURABLE POWER OF ATTORNEY THAT BECOMES EFFECTIVE ON YOUR INCAPACITY AS HEREAFTER SET FORTH. BEFORE EXECUTING THIS DOCUMENT, YOU SHOULD KNOW THESE IMPORTANT FACTS.

1. THIS DOCUMENT MAY PROVIDE THE PERSON YOU DESIGNATE AS YOUR ATTORNEY-IN-FACT WITH BROAD POWERS TO DISPOSE, SELL, CONVEY, AND ENCUMBER YOUR REAL AND PERSONAL PROPERTY.

2. THESE POWERS WILL EXIST FOR AN INDEFINITE PERIOD OF TIME UNLESS YOU LIMIT THEIR DURATION IN THIS DOCUMENT. THESE POWERS WILL CONTINUE TO EXIST NOTWITHSTANDING YOUR SUBSEQUENT DISABILITY OR INCAPACITY.

3. YOU HAVE THE RIGHT TO REVOKE OR TERMINATE THIS DURABLE POWER OF ATTORNEY AT ANY TIME.

POWER OF ATTORNEY TO BECOME EFFECTIVE ONLY ON INCAPACITY OF PRINCIPAL

This durable power of attorney shall become effective only on the incapacity of the undersigned principal. The undersigned shall conclusively be deemed incapacitated for purposes of this instrument when the agent receives a written and signed opinion from a licensed physician that the principal is physically or mentally incapable of managing the principal's finances. Such written opinion, when received, shall be attached to this instrument. Third parties may rely on the agent's authority without further evidence of incapacity when this instrument is presented with such physician's statement attached. No licensed physician who executes a medical opinion of incapacity shall be subject to liability because of such execution. The principal hereby waives any privilege that may apply to release of information included in such medical opinion.

While the principal is not incapacitated, this durable power of attorney may be modified by the principal at any time by written notice given by the principal to the agent and may be terminated at any time by either the principal or the agent by written notice given by the terminating party to the other party.

This power of attorney shall continue after the principal's incapacity in accordance with its terms.

On the death of the principal, this power shall terminate and the assets of the principal shall be distributed to the duly appointed personal representative of the principal's estate; or, if no estate is being administered, to the persons who lawfully take the assets without the necessity of administration when they have supplied the agent with satisfactory documents as provided by law.

TO WHOM IT MAY CONCERN:

Ⓐ _____, the principal, presently a resident of
_____ County, state of _____, hereby appoints
Ⓑ_____, presently a resident of _____ County,
state of _____, as the principal's true and lawful attorney-in-fact for the
principal and in the principal's name, place, and stead on the principal's incapacity:

1. To manage, control, lease, sublease, and otherwise act concerning any real property that the principal may own, collect and receive rents or income therefrom, pay taxes, charges, and assessments on the same, repair, maintain, protect, preserve, alter, and improve the same and do all things necessary or expedient to be done in the agent's judgment in connection with the property.

2. To manage and control all partnership interests owned by the principal and to make all decisions the principal could make as a general partner, limited partner, or both, and to execute all documents required of the principal as such partner, all to the extent that the agent's designation for such purposes is allowed by law and is not in contravention of any partnership or other agreement.

3. To purchase, sell, invest, reinvest, and generally deal with all stocks, bonds, debentures, warrants, partnership interests, rights, and securities owned by the principal.

4. To collect and deposit for the benefit of the principal all debts, interest, dividends, or other assets that may be due or belong to the principal and to execute and deliver receipts and other discharges therefore; to demand, arbitrate, and pursue litigation on the principal's behalf concerning all rights and benefits to which the principal may be entitled; and to compromise, settle, and discharge all such matters as the agent considers appropriate under the circumstances.

5. To pay any sums of money that may at any time is or become owing from the principal, to sell, and to adjust and compromise any claims which may be made against the principal as the agent considers appropriate under the circumstances.

6. To grant, sell, transfer, mortgage, deed in trust, pledge and otherwise deal in all property, real and personal, that the principal may own, including but not limited to any real property described on any exhibit attached to this instrument including property acquired after execution of this instrument; to attach exhibits to this instrument that provide legal descriptions of all such property; and to execute such instruments as the agent deems proper in conjunction with all matters covered in this paragraph 6.

7. To prepare and file all income and other federal and state tax returns that the principal is required to file; to sign the principal's name; hire preparers and advisors and pay for their services; and to do whatever is necessary to protect the principal's assets from assessments for income taxes and other taxes to receive confidential information; to receive checks in payment of any refund of taxes, penalties, or interest; to execute waivers (including offers of waivers) of restrictions on assessment or collection of tax deficiencies and waivers of notice of disallowance of claims for credit or refund; to execute consents extending the statutory period for assessment or collection of taxes; to execute closing agreements under Internal Revenue Code section 7121 or any successor statute; and to delegate authority or substitute another representative with respect to all above matters.

8. To deposit in and draw on any checking, savings, agency, or other accounts that the principal may have in any banks, savings and loan associations, and any accounts with securities brokers or other commercial institutions, and to establish and terminate all such accounts.

9. To invest and reinvest the principal's funds in every kind of property, real, personal, or mixed, and every kind of investment, specifically including, but not limited to, corporate obligations of every kind, preferred or common stocks, shares of investment trusts, investment companies, and mutual funds, and mortgage participations that, under the circumstances then prevailing (specifically including but not limited to the general economic conditions and the principal's anticipated needs), persons of skill, prudence, and diligence acting in a similar capacity and familiar with those matters would use in the conduct of an enterprise of a similar character and with similar aims, to attain the principal's goals; and to consider individual investments as part of an overall plan.

10. To have access to all safe-deposit boxes in the principal's name or to which the principal is an authorized signatory; to contract with financial institutions for the maintenance and continuation of safe-deposit boxes in the principal's name; to add to and remove the contents of all such safe-deposit boxes; and to terminate contracts for all such safe-deposit boxes.

11. To make additions and transfer assets to any and all living revocable trusts of which the principal is a settlor.

12. To make direct payments to the provider for tuition and medical care for the principal's issue under Internal Revenue Code section 3503(e) or any successor statute, which excludes such payments from gift tax liability.

13. To use any credit cards in the principal's name to make purchases and to sign charge slips on behalf of the principal as may be required to use such credit cards; and to close the principal's charge accounts and terminate the principal's credit cards under circumstances where the agent considers such acts to be in the principal's best interest.

14. Generally to do, execute, and perform any other act, deed, matter, or thing, that in the opinion of the agent ought to be done, executed, or performed in conjunction with this power of attorney, of every kind and nature, as fully and effectively as the principal could do if personally present. The enumeration of specific items, acts, rights, or powers does not limit or restrict, and is not to be construed or interpreted as limiting or restricting, the general powers granted to the agent except where powers are expressly restricted.

15. The agent is authorized and directed to commence enforcement proceedings, at the principal's expense, against any third party who fails to honor this durable power of attorney.

16. Notwithstanding any other possible language to the contrary in this document, the agent is specifically NOT granted the following powers:

(a) To use the principal's assets for the agent's own legal obligations, including but not limited to support of the agent's dependents;

(b) To exercise any trustee powers under an irrevocable trust of which the agent is a settlor and the principal is a trustee; and,

(c) To exercise incidents of ownership over any life insurance policies that the principal owns on the agent's life.

17. Any third party from whom the agent may request information, records, or other documents regarding the principal's personal affairs may release and deliver all such information, records, or documents to the agent. The principal hereby waives any privilege that may apply to release of such information, records, or other documents.

18. The agent's signature under the authority granted in this power of attorney may be accepted by any third party or organization with the same force and effect as if the principal were personally present and acting on the principal's own behalf. No person or organization who relies on the agent's authority under this instrument shall incur any liability to the principal, the principal's estate, heirs, successors, or assigns, because of reliance on this instrument.

19. The principal's estate, heirs, successors, and assigns shall be bound by the agent's acts under this power of attorney.

20. This power of attorney shall commence and take effect on the principal's subsequent disability or incapacity as set forth above.

21. The principal hereby ratifies and confirms all that the agent shall do, or cause to be done, by virtue of this power of attorney.

22. If the named attorney-in-fact is for any reason unwilling or unable so to serve, then the principal hereby nominates Ⓒ _____, presently a resident of _____ County, state of _____, as the principal's true and lawful attorney-in-fact.

23. If a conservatorship of the principal's person or estate or both is deemed necessary, the principal hereby nominates Ⓓ _____ as conservator of the principal's person and estate. If _____ is for any reason unwilling or unable so to serve, the principal hereby nominates _____ as such conservator.

On the appointment of a conservator of the principal's estate, this power of attorney shall terminate and the agent shall deliver the assets of the principal under the agent's control as directed by the conservator of the principal's estate.

Ⓔ IN WITNESS WHEREOF, the principal has signed this springing durable power of attorney on _____.

_____
(Signature)

Ⓕ STATE OF _____
   COUNTY OF _____

On this _____ day of _____, 200____, before me, _____, a notary public in and for said county and state, residing herein, duly commissioned and sworn, personally appeared _____ personally known to me (or proved to me on the basis of satisfactory evidence) to be the person whose name is subscribed to the within instrument and acknowledged to me that he/she executed the same in his/her authorized capacity, and that by his/her signature on the instrument the person, or entity upon behalf of which the person acted, executed the instrument.

WITNESS my hand and official seal.

_____
(Signature of Notary Public)

PERSONAL DATA AND RECORD LOCATOR

PERSONAL DATA
Social Security Number _____ - _____ - _____
Phone Number _____
Email Address _____@_____
Fax Number _____
Driver's License Number _____

PROPOSED GUARDIAN OF MINOR CHILD/CHILDREN
Name _____
Address _____
Phone Number _____
Relationship to Child/Children _____

LEGAL AND FINANCIAL ADVISORS
Name of Attorney _____
Phone Number _____
Name of Accountant _____
Phone Number _____
Name of Trustee/Executor _____
Phone Number _____
Name of Insurance Agent _____
Phone Number _____
Name of Financial Advisor/Stockbroker _____
Phone Number _____

LOCATION OF DOCUMENTS
Personal Address Book _____
Estate Planning Documents (Will, Trust, Living Will, Powers of Attorney,
Legacy Will) _____
Organ Donor Cards _____
Deeds/Titles to Real Estate and Personal Property _____
Income Tax Records _____
Vital Statistics (Birth Certificate, Marriage License, Military Records)
_____
Funeral/Cemetery Contracts _____
Medical Records _____
Insurance Policies _____
Investment Certificates (Stocks, Bonds, 401K, IRA, Pension, Etc.)
_____
Vehicle (Auto/RV/Boat) Registration _____
Bank Statements _____
Credit Card Records _____
Insurance Policies _____
Extra Keys _____
Pet Records _____

Contracts _____
Home Repair/Warranties _____
Vehicle Maintenance _____
Frequent Flyer Miles _____
Passports/Social Security Cards _____
Unfinished Business (Leases, Contracts, Moneys Owed to You) _____
_____
Location of Home Safe _____
Ongoing Divorce or Other Court Proceedings/Judgments _____
_____
Trademarks, Copyrights, Patents, and Other Important Papers _____
_____
Safe-Deposit Records _____
Location of Key to Safe-Deposit Box _____
_____ at _____ Bank

PERSONAL COMPUTER ACCESSIBILITY
Screen Name _____
Password _____

EMPLOYMENT
Name of Employer _____
Phone Number _____
Immediate Supervisor _____
Benefits Dept. Phone Number _____

PERSONS TO NOTIFY UPON DEATH
Name _____ Phone Number _____
Name _____ Phone Number _____
Name _____ Phone Number _____
Name _____ Phone Number _____

ORGANIZATIONS TO BE NOTIFIED UPON DEATH
Name _____
Phone Number _____
Contact Person _____

Name _____
Phone Number _____
Contact Person _____

Name _____
Phone Number _____
Contact Person _____

ACCOUNTS ORGANIZER

List All Non-Tax-Deferred Accounts (Savings, Checking, Credit Union, Brokerage, CDs, Treasury Bills, Other)

Name	Value	Account #
_____	_____	_____
_____	_____	_____
_____	_____	_____
_____	_____	_____

List All Tax-Deferred Accounts (IRA, 401(k), Pension, Profit, Sharing, Keoghs, Tax-Deferred Annuities, Other)

Name	Value	Account #
_____	_____	_____
_____	_____	_____
_____	_____	_____
_____	_____	_____

List All Insurance Benefits (Military, Life, Home, Disability, Long-Term Care, Medical, Auto, Other)

Company	Policy #	Beneficiary
_____	_____	_____
_____	_____	_____
_____	_____	_____
_____	_____	_____

FREQUENT FLYER MILES

Many frequent flyer programs allow you to transfer miles in to your spouse and other family members. The airlines will require a copy of a death certificate and written documentation from you assigning the miles in your account. You can make written provision for the transfer in your Will or Trust.

Name of Airline Program	Account #	Customer Service #
_____	_____	_____
_____	_____	_____
_____	_____	_____
_____	_____	_____

List All Obligations (Home, Vacation Home, Time-Share, Automobile, Boat, Motorcycle, RV Loans, Bank Credit Cards, Department Stores, Other)

Name	Account #	Customer Service #

List All Checking Account Automatic Deductions (Internet, Cable, Satellite, Cell Phone, Newspapers, Insurance, Fitness Club, and Other Memberships)

Name	Account #	Customer Service #

SCHEDULE OF DEBTS

INSTRUCTIONS:

Please list all of your debts that are not paid in full. Under the heading "Type of Debt," describe the type of debt by entering the appropriate letter found in the key section.

KEY:

Automobile and Other Vehicles   (A)
Credit Cards   (C)
Medical   (M)
Real Estate   (R)
Other   (O)

NAME: _____

SSN: _____

Name of Creditor	Account #	Type of Debt	Balance Owed

HOME MAINTENANCE AND EMERGENCY WORKSHEET

PROVIDE THE NAME AND PHONE NUMBER FOR EACH OF THE FOLLOWING:

Air Conditioning/Heating _____

Security/Alarm Service Security Code/password _____

_____

Gate/Apartment Manager _____

Appliance Repair _____

Gardener _____

Pool Service _____

Cleaning Service _____

Plumber _____

Window Cleaning _____

Utility Companies

    Electric _____

    Gas _____

    Phone _____

    Trash _____

    Water _____

Cable/Satellite _____

Newspaper _____

Magazines/Other Publications _____

_____

IN CASE OF AN EMERGENCY, PLEASE IDENTIFY THE LOCATION IN YOUR HOME OF THE FOLLOWING:

Gas Meter _____

Electrical Breaker Panel _____

Sprinkler Control Panel _____

Security Alarm Panel _____

Water Meter _____

Water Shut-Off Valve _____

Air Conditioner _____

Water Heater _____

INDEX

D

G

H

T

U

V

W

X

Y

ABOUT
THE AUTHOR

Benjamin Berkley has practiced law for more than twenty-eight years, specializing in estate planning and estate administration. He earned his law degree from Western State University. In addition to being admitted to the State Bar of California and the United States Supreme Court, he is also licensed by the State of California and the Department of Justice as a private fiduciary for court appointments as a conservator and trustee of estates.

Mr. Berkley also serves as a panel referral attorney for the nation's largest prepaid legal programs, including ARAG Legal, Hyatt Legal, and GE Consumer Signature Legal. He is a network attorney for AARP members. He regularly conducts seminars on estate planning and has become an advocate for senior rights.

Ben lives with his wife and two children in southern California.

Sphinx® Publishing's National Titles
Valid in All 50 States

LEGAL SURVIVAL IN BUSINESS

The Complete Book of Corporate Forms (2E)	$29.95
The Complete Hiring and Firing Handbook	$19.95
The Complete Limited Liability Kit	$24.95
The Complete Partnership Book	$24.95
The Complete Patent Book	$26.95
The Complete Patent Kit	$39.95
The Entrepreneur's Internet Handbook	$21.95
The Entrepreneur's Legal Guide	$26.95
Financing Your Small Business	$16.95
Fired, Laid-Off or Forced Out	$14.95
Form Your Own Corporation (5E)	$29.95
The Home-Based Business Kit	$14.95
How to Buy a Franchise	$19.95
How to Form a Nonprofit Corporation (3E)	$24.95
How to Register Your Own Copyright (5E)	$24.95
HR for Small Business	$14..95
Incorporate in Delaware from Any State	$26.95
Incorporate in Nevada from Any State	$24.95
The Law (In Plain English)® for Restaurants	$16.95
The Law (In Plain English)® for Small Business	$19.95
The Law (In Plain English)® for Writers	$14.95
Making Music Your Business	$18.95
Minding Her Own Business (4E)	$14.95
Most Valuable Business Legal Forms You'll Ever Need (3E)	$21.95
Profit from Intellectual Property	$28.95
Protect Your Patent	$24.95
The Small Business Owner's Guide to Bankruptcy	$21.95
Start Your Own Law Practice	$16.95
Tax Power for the Self-Eemployed	$17.95
Tax Smarts for Small Business	$21.95
Your Rights at Work	$14.95

LEGAL SURVIVAL IN COURT

Attorney Responsibilities & Client Rights	$19.95
Crime Victim's Guide to Justice (2E)	$21.95
Legal Research Made Easy (4E)	$24.95
Winning Your Personal Injury Claim (3E)	$24.95

LEGAL SURVIVAL IN REAL ESTATE

The Complete Kit to Selling Your Own Home	$18.95
The Complete Book of Real Estate Contracts	$18.95
Essential Guide to Real Estate Leases	$18.95
Homeowner's Rights	$19.95
How to Buy a Condominium or Townhome (2E)	$19.95
How to Buy Your First Home (2E)	$14.95
How to Make Money on Foreclosures	$16.95
The Mortgage Answer Book	$14.95
Sell Your Own Home Without a Broker	$14.95
The Weekend Landlord	$16.95
The Weekend Real Estate Investor	$14.95
Working with Your Homeowners Association	$19.95

LEGAL SURVIVAL IN SPANISH

Cómo Comprar su Primera Casa	$8.95
Cómo Conseguir Trabajo en los Estados Unidos	$8.95
Cómo Hacer su Propio Testamento	$16.95
Cómo Iniciar su Propio Negocio	$8.95
Cómo Negociar su Crédito	$8.95
Cómo Organizar un Presupuesto	$8.95
Cómo Solicitar su Propio Divorcio	$24.95
Guía de Inmigración a Estados Unidos (4E)	$24.95
Guía de Justicia para Víctimas del Crimen	$21.95
Guía Esencial para los Contratos de Arrendamiento de Bienes Raices	$22.95
Inmigración y Ciudadanía en los EE.UU. Preguntas y Respuestas	$16.95
Inmigración a los EE.UU. Paso a Paso (2E)	$24.95
Manual de Beneficios del Seguro Social	$18.95
El Seguro Social Preguntas y Respuestas	$16.95
¡Visas! ¡Visas! ¡Visas!	$9.95

LEGAL SURVIVAL IN PERSONAL AFFAIRS

101 Complaint Letters That Get Results	$18.95
The 529 College Savings Plan (2E)	$18.95
The 529 College Savings Plan Made Simple	$7.95
The Alternative Minimum Tax	$14.95
The Antique and Art Collector's Legal Guide	$24.95
The Childcare Answer Book	$12.95
Child Support	$18.95
The Complete Book of Insurance	$18.95
The Complete Book of Personal Legal Forms	$24.95
The Complete Credit Repair Kit	$19.95
The Complete Legal Guide to Senior Care	$21.95
The Complete Personal Bankruptcy Guide	$21.95
Credit Smart	$18.95
The Easy Will and Living Will Kit	$16.95
Fathers' Rights	$19.95
File Your Own Divorce (6E)	$24.95
The Frequent Traveler's Guide	$14.95
Gay & Lesbian Rights (2E)	$21.95
Grandparents' Rights (4E)	$24.95
How to Parent with Your Ex	$12.95
How to Write Your Own Living Will (4E)	$18.95
How to Write Your Own Premarital Agreement (3E)	$24.95
The Infertility Answer Book	$16.95
Law 101	$16.95
Law School 101	$16.95
The Living Trust Kit	$21.95
Living Trusts and Other Ways to Avoid Probate (3E)	$24.95
Make Your Own Simple Will (4E)	$26.95
Mastering the MBE	$16.95
Money and Divorce	$14.95
My Wishes	@1.95
Nursing Homes and Assisted Living Facilities	$19.95
Power of Attorney Handbook (6E)	$24.95
Quick Cash	$14.95
Seniors' Rights	$19.95
Sexual Harassment in the Workplace	$18.95
Sexual Harassment:Your Guide to Legal Action	$18.95
Sisters-in-Law	$16.95
The Social Security Benefits Handbook (4E)	$18.95
Social Security Q&A	$12.95
Starting Out or Starting Over	$14.95
Teen Rights (and Responsibilities) (2E)	$14.95
Unmarried Parents' Rights (and Responsibilities)(3E)	$16.95
U.S. Immigration and Citizenship Q&A	$18.95
U.S. Immigration Step by Step (2E)	$24.95
U.S.A. Immigration Guide (5E)	$26.95
What They Don't Teach You in College	$12.95
What to Do—Before "I DO"	$14.95
The Wills and Trusts Kit (2E)	$29.95
Win Your Unemployment Compensation Claim (2E)	$21.95
Your Right to Child Custody, Visitation and Support (3E)	$24.95

SPHINX® PUBLISHING ORDER FORM

BILL TO:		SHIP TO:	
Phone #	**Terms**	**F.O.B.** Chicago, IL	**Ship Date**

Charge my: ☐ VISA ☐ MasterCard ☐ American Express

☐ **Money Order or Personal Check**

Credit Card Number

Expiration Date

Qty	ISBN	Title	Retail	Ext.	Qty	ISBN	Title	Retail	Ext.
		SPHINX PUBLISHING NATIONAL TITLES				1-57248-520-5	How to Make Money on Foreclosures	$16.95	
	1-57248-363-6	101 Complaint Letters That Get Results	$18.95			1-57248-479-9	How to Parent with Your Ex	$12.95	
	1-57248-361-X	The 529 College Savings Plan (2E)	$18.95			1-57248-379-2	How to Register Your Own Copyright (5E)	$24.95	
	1-57248-483-7	The 529 College Savings Plan Made Simple	$7.95			1-57248-394-6	How to Write Your Own Living Will (4E)	$18.95	
	1-57248-460-8	The Alternative Minimum Tax	$14.95			1-57248-156-0	How to Write Your Own Premarital Agreement (3E)	$24.95	
	1-57248-349-0	The Antique and Art Collector's Legal Guide	$24.95			1-57248-504-3	HR for Small Business	$14.95	
	1-57248-347-4	Attorney Responsibilities & Client Rights	$19.95			1-57248-230-3	Incorporate in Delaware from Any State	$26.95	
	1-57248-482-9	The Childcare Answer Book	$12.95			1-57248-158-7	Incorporate in Nevada from Any State	$24.95	
	1-57248-382-2	Child Support	$18.95			1-57248-531-0	The Infertility Answer Book	$16.95	
	1-57248-487-X	Cómo Comprar su Primera Casa	$8.95			1-57248-474-8	Inmigración a los EE.UU. Paso a Paso (2E)	$24.95	
	1-57248-488-8	Cómo Conseguir Trabajo en los Estados Unidos	$8.95			1-57248-400-4	Inmigración y Ciudadanía en los EE.UU.	$16.95	
	1-57248-148-X	Cómo Hacer su Propio Testamento	$16.95				Preguntas y Respuestas		
	1-57248-532-9	Cómo Iniciar su Propio Negocio	$8.95			1-57248-453-5	Law 101	$16.95	
	1-57248-462-4	Cómo Negociar su Crédito	$8.95			1-57248-374-1	Law School 101	$16.95	
	1-57248-463-2	Cómo Organizar un Presupuesto	$8.95			1-57248-523-X	The Law (In Plain English)® for Restaurants	$16.95	
	1-57248-147-1	Cómo Solicitar su Propio Divorcio	$24.95			1-57248-377-6	The Law (In Plain English)® for Small Business	$19.95	
	1-57248-507-8	The Complete Book of Corporate Forms (2E)	$29.95			1-57248-476-4	The Law (In Plain English)® for Writers	$14.95	
	1-57248-383-0	The Complete Book of Insurance	$18.95			1-57248-509-4	Legal Research Made Easy (4E)	$24.95	
	1-57248499-3	The Complete Book of Personal Legal Forms	$24.95			1-57248-449-7	The Living Trust Kit	$21.95	
	1-57248-528-0	The Complete Book of Real Estate Contracts	$18.95			1-57248-165-X	Living Trusts and Other Ways to	$24.95	
	1-57248-500-0	The Complete Credit Repair Kit	$19.95				Avoid Probate (3E)		
	1-57248-458-6	The Complete Hiring and Firing Handbook	$18.95			1-57248-511-6	Make Your Own Simple Will (4E)	$26.95	
	1-57248-484-5	The Complete Home-Based Business Kit	$16.95			1-57248-486-1	Making Music Your Business	$18.95	
	1-57248-353-9	The Complete Kit to Selling Your Own Home	$18.95			1-57248-186-2	Manual de Beneficios para el Seguro Social	$18.95	
	1-57248-229-X	The Complete Legal Guide to Senior Care	$21.95			1-57248-220-6	Mastering the MBE	$16.95	
	1-57248-498-5	The Complete Limited Liability Company Kit	$24.95			1-57248-455-1	Minding Her Own Business, 4E	$14.95	
	1-57248-391-1	The Complete Partnership Book	$24.95			1-57248-524-8	Money and Divorce	$14.95	
	1-57248-201-X	The Complete Patent Book	$26.95			1-57248-480-2	The Mortgage Answer Book	$14.95	
	1-57248-514-0	The Complete Patent Kit	$39.95			1-57248-167-6	Most Val. Business Legal Forms	$21.95	
	1-57248-545-0	The Complete Personal Bankruptcy Guide	$21.95				You'll Ever Need (3E)		
	1-57248-480-2	The Mortgage Answer Book	$14.95			1-57248-519-1	My Wishes	$21.95	
	1-57248-369-5	Credit Smart	$18.95			1-57248-535-3	Power of Attorney Handbook (6E)	$24.95	
	1-57248-163-3	Crime Victim's Guide to Justice (2E)	$21.95			1-57248-332-6	Profit from Intellectual Property	$28.95	
	1-57248-481-0	The Easy Will and Living Will Kit	$16.95			1-57248-329-6	Protect Your Patent	$24.95	
	1-57248-251-6	The Entrepreneur's Internet Handbook	$21.95			1-57248-376-8	Nursing Homes and Assisted Living Facilities	$19.95	
	1-57248-235-4	The Entrepreneur's Legal Guide	$26.95			1-57248-385-7	Quick Cash	$14.95	
	1-57248-160-9	Essential Guide to Real Estate Leases	$18.95			1-57248-350-4	El Seguro Social Preguntas y Respuestas	$16.95	
	1-57248-375-X	Fathers' Rights	$19.95			1-57248-529-9	Sell Your Home Without a Broker	$14.95	
	1-57248-517-5	File Your Own Divorce (6E)	$24.95			1-57248386-5	Seniors' Rights	$19.95	
	1-57248-553-1	Financing Your Small Business	$16.95			1-57248-527-2	Sexual Harassment in the Workplace	$18.95	
	1-57248-459-4	Fired, Laid Off or Forced Out	$14.95			1-57248-217-6	Sexual Harassment: Your Guide to Legal Action	$18.95	
	1-57248-516-7	Form Your Own Corporation (4E)	$29.95			1-57248-378-4	Sisters-in-Law	$16.95	
	1-57248-502-7	The Frequent Traveler's Guide	$14.95			1-57248-219-2	The Small Business Owner's Guide to Bankruptcy	$21.95	
	1-57248-550-7	Gay & Lesbian Rights (2E)	$21.95			1-57248-395-4	The Social Security Benefits Handbook (4E)	$18.95	
	1-57248-526-4	Grandparents' Rights (4E)	$24.95			1-57248-216-8	Social Security Q&A	$12.95	
	1-57248-475-6	Guía de Inmigración a Estados Unidos (4E)	$24.95			1-57248-521-3	Start Your Own Law Practice	$16.95	
	1-57248-187-0	Guía de Justicia para Víctimas del Crimen	$21.95			1-57248-328-8	Starting Out or Starting Over	$14.95	
	1-57248-253-2	Guía Esencial para los Contratos de	$22.95			1-57248-525-6	Teen Rlghts (and Responsibilities) (2E)	$14.95	
		Arrendamiento de Bienes Raices				1-57248-457-8	Tax Power for the Self-Employed	$17.95	
	1-57248-334-2	Homeowner's Rights	$19.95			1-57248-366-0	Tax Smarts for Small Business	$21.95	
	1-57248-164-1	How to Buy a Condominium or Townhome (2E)	$19.95			1-57248-530-2	Unmarried Parents' Rights (3E)	$16.95	
	1-57248-197-7	How to Buy Your First Home (2E)	$14.95			1-57248-362-8	U.S. Immigration and Citizenship Q&A	$18.95	
	1-57248-384-9	How to Buy a Franchise	$19.95			1-57248-387-3	U.S. Immigration Step by Step (2E)	$24.95	
	1-57248-390-3	How to Form a Nonprofit Corporation (3E)	$24.95			1-57248-392-X	U.S.A. Immigration Guide (5E)	$26.95	

(Form Continued on Following Page)   **Subtotal** _____

To order, call Sourcebooks at 1-800-432-7444 or FAX (630) 961-2168 (Bookstores, libraries, wholesalers—please call for discount)

Prices are subject to change without notice.

Find more legal information at: **www.SphinxLegal.com**

SPHINX® PUBLISHING ORDER FORM

Qty	ISBN	Title	Retail	Ext.
___	1-57248-178-0	¡Visas! ¡Visas! ¡Visas!	$9.95	___
___	1-57248-554-X	What They Don't Teach You in College	$12.95	___
___	1-57248-177-2	The Weekend Landlord	$16.95	___
___	1-57248-557-4	The Weekend Real Estate Investor	$14.95	___
___	1-57248-451-9	What to Do—Before "I DO"	$14.95	___
___	1-57248-225-7	Win Your Unemployment Compensation Claim (2E)	$21.95	___
___	1-57248-518-3	The Wills and Trusts Kit	$29.95	___
___	1-57248-473-X	Winning Your Personal Injury Claim (3E)	$24.95	___
___	1-57248-333-4	Working with Your Homeowners Association	$19.95	___
___	1-57248-380-6	Your Right to Child Custody, Visitation and Support (3E)	$24.95	___
___	1-57248-505-1	Your Rights at Work	$14.95	___
		CALIFORNIA TITLES		
___	1-57248-489-6	How to File for Divorce in CA (5E)	$26.95	___
___	1-57248-464-0	How to Settle and Probate an Estate in CA (2E)	$28.95	___
___	1-57248-336-9	How to Start a Business in CA (2E)	$21.95	___
___	1-57248-194-3	How to Win in Small Claims Court in CA (2E)	$18.95	___
___	1-57248-246-X	Make Your Own CA Will	$18.95	___
___	1-57248-397-0	Landlords' Legal Guide in CA (2E)	$24.95	___
___	1-57248-515-9	Tenants' Rights in CA (2E)	$24.95	___
		FLORIDA TITLES		
___	1-57248-396-2	How to File for Divorce in FL (8E)	$28.95	___
___	1-57248-490-X	How to Form a Limited Liability Co. in FL (4E)	$24.95	___
___	1-57071-401-0	How to Form a Partnership in FL	$22.95	___
___	1-57248-456-X	How to Make a FL Will (7E)	$16.95	___
___	1-57248-204-4	How to Win in Small Claims Court in FL (7E)	$18.95	___
___	1-57248-540-X	Incorporate in FL (7E)	$29.95	___
___	1-57248-381-4	Land Trusts in Florida (7E)	$29.95	___
___	1-57248-491-8	Landlords' Rights and Duties in FL (10E)	$24.95	___
___	1-57248-558-2	Probate and Settle an Estate in FL (6E)	$29.95	___
___	1-57248-538-8	Start a Business in FL (8E)	$29.95	___
		GEORGIA TITLES		
___	1-57248-340-7	How to File for Divorce in GA (5E)	$21.95	___
___	1-57248-493-4	How to Start a Business in GA (4E)	$21.95	___
		ILLINOIS TITLES		
___	1-57248-244-3	Child Custody, Visitation, and Support in IL	$24.95	___
___	1-57248-510-8	File for Divorce in IL (4E)	$26.95	___
___	1-57248-170-6	How to Make an IL Will (3E)	$16.95	___
___	1-57248-265-9	How to Start a Business in IL (4E)	$21.95	___
___	1-57248-252-4	Landlords' Legal Guide in IL	$24.95	___
		MARYLAND, VIRGINIA AND THE DISTRICT OF COLUMBIA		
___	1-57248-240-0	How to File for Divorce in MD, VA, and DC	$28.95	___
___	1-57248-359-8	How to Start a Business in MD, VA, or DC	$21.95	___
		MASSACHUSETTS TITLES		
___	1-57248-115-3	How to Form a Corporation in MA	$24.95	___
___	1-57248-466-7	How to Start a Business in MA (4E)	$21.95	___
___	1-57248-398-9	Landlords' Legal Guide in MA (2E)	$24.95	___
		MICHIGAN TITLES		
___	1-57248-467-5	How to File for Divorce in MI (4E)	$24.95	___
___	1-57248-182-X	How to Make a MI Will (3E)	$16.95	___
___	1-57248-468-3	How to Start a Business in MI (4E)	$18.95	___
		MINNESOTA TITLES		
___	1-57248-142-0	How to File for Divorce in MN	$21.95	___
___	1-57248-179-X	How to Form a Corporation in MN	$24.95	___
___	1-57248-178-1	How to Make a MN Will (2E)	$16.95	___

Qty	ISBN	Title	Retail	Ext
		NEW JERSEY TITLES		
___	1-57248-512-4	File for Divorce in NJ (2E)	$24.95	___
___	1-57248-448-9	How to Start a Business in NJ	$21.95	___
		NEW YORK TITLES		
___	1-57248-193-5	Child Custody, Visitation and Support in NY	$26.95	___
___	1-57248-351-2	File for Divorce in NY	$26.95	___
___	1-57248-249-4	How to Form a Corporation in NY (2E)	$24.95	___
___	1-57248-401-2	How to Make a NY Will (3E)	$16.95	___
___	1-57248-469-1	How to Start a Business in NY (3E)	$21.95	___
___	1-57248-198-6	How to Win in Small Claims Court in NY (2E)	$18.95	___
___	1-57248-122-6	Tenants' Rights in NY	$21.95	___
		NORTH CAROLINA AND SOUTH CAROLINA TITLES		
___	1-57248-508-6	How to File for Divorce in NC (4E)	$26.95	___
___	1-57248-371-7	How to Start a Business in NC or SC	$24.95	___
___	1-57248-091-2	Landlords' Rights & Duties in NC	$21.95	___
		OHIO TITLES		
___	1-57248-503-5	How to File for Divorce in OH (3E)	$24.95	___
___	1-57248-174-9	How to Form a Corporation in OH	$24.95	___
___	1-57248-173-0	How to Make an OH Will	$16.95	___
		PENNSYLVANIA TITLES		
___	1-57248-242-7	Child Custody, Visitation and Support in PA	$26.95	___
___	1-57248-495-0	How to File for Divorce in PA (4E)	$24.95	___
___	1-57248-358-X	How to Form a Corporation in PA	$24.95	___
___	1-57248-094-7	How to Make a PA Will (2E)	$16.95	___
___	1-57248-357-1	How to Start a Business in PA (3E)	$21.95	___
___	1-57248-245-1	Landlords' Legal Guide in PA	$24.95	___
		TEXAS TITLES		
___	1-57248-171-4	Child Custody, Visitation, and Support in TX	$22.95	___
___	1-57248-399-7	How to File for Divorce in TX (4E)	$24.95	___
___	1-57248-470-5	How to Form a Corporation in TX (3E)	$24.95	___
___	1-57248-496-9	How to Probate and Settle an Estate in TX (4E)	$26.95	___
___	1-57248-471-3	How to Start a Business in TX (4E)	$21.95	___
___	1-57248-111-0	How to Win in Small Claims Court in TX (2E)	$16.95	___
___	1-57248-355-5	Landlords' Legal Guide in TX	$24.95	___
___	1-57248-513-2	Write Your Own TX Will (4E)	$16.95	___
		WASHINGTON TITLES		
___	1-57248-522-1	File for Divorce in WA	$24.95	___

SubTotal This page ___

SubTotal previous page ___

Shipping— $5.00 for 1st book, $1.00 each additional ___

Illinois residents add 6.75% sales tax ___

Connecticut residents add 6.00% sales tax ___

Total ___

To order, call Sourcebooks at 1-800-432-7444 or FAX (630) 961-2168 (Bookstores, libraries, wholesalers—please call for discount)

Prices are subject to change without notice.

Find more legal information at: **www.SphinxLegal.com**